Microwave
WHOLEFOOD

BRAMLEY BOOKS

Recipes Compiled by Nina Morgan
Edited by Judith Ferguson
Prepared and Styled by Jacqueline Bellefontaine
Photographed by Peter Barry
Designed by Sara Cooper
Produced by David Gibbon,
    Gerald Hughes and Ted Smart

CLB 1842
This edition published 1986 by Bramley Books, Godalming, Surrey.
© 1987 Colour Library Books Ltd., Guildford, Surrey.
Printed and bound in Barcelona, Spain by Cronion, S.A.
All rights reserved.
ISBN 0-86283-572-0

Acknowledgement
Microwave ovens used for testing and preparation for
photography supplied by Samsung Electronics (UK) Ltd.
Cookware and accessories provided by Lakeland Plastics
of Windermere, Cumbria. Pyrex and microwave cookware
dishes supplied by Corning Ltd.

CONTENTS

GENERAL INTRODUCTION

People are usually of two minds about microwave ovens. Experienced cooks are sceptical. Inexperienced cooks are mystified. Most people who don't own one think a microwave oven is an expensive luxury. Those of us who have one, though, would find it difficult to give it up. Great advances have been made in the design and capabilities of microwave ovens since the demand for them first began in the Sixties. With so many kinds of ovens available, both beginners and advanced cooks can find one that best suits their particular needs.

How Microwave Ovens Work

Microwave ovens, whatever the make or model, do have certain things in common. The energy that makes fast cooking possible is comprised of electromagnetic waves converted from electricity. Microwaves are a type of high frequency radio wave. The waves are of short length, hence the name microwave.

Inside the oven is a magnetron, which converts ordinary electricity into microwaves. A wave guide channels the microwaves into the oven cavity, and a stirrer fan circulates them evenly. Microwaves are attracted to the particles of moisture that form part of any food. As the microwaves are absorbed, to a depth of about 4-5cm/1½-2 inches, they cause the water molecules in the food to vibrate, about 2000 million times a second. This generates the heat that cooks the food. The heat reaches the centre of the food by conduction, just as in ordinary cooking. However, this is accomplished much faster than in conventional cooking because no heat is generated until the waves are absorbed by the food. All the energy is concentrated on cooking the food and not on heating the oven itself or the baking dishes. Standing time is often necessary to allow the food to continue cooking after it is removed from the oven.

Most microwave ovens have an ON indicator light and a timer control. Some timer controls look like minute timers, while others are calibrated in seconds up to 50 seconds and minutes up to 30 minutes. This can vary slightly; some models have a 10 minute interval setting. Some ovens have a separate ON-OFF switch, while others switch on with the timer or power setting. Almost all have a bell or buzzer to signal the end of cooking time.

Microwave Oven Features

At this point, things really begin to diversify. Different terms are used for the same power setting depending on what brand of oven you buy. Some ovens have a wider range of different settings as well. Chart No. 1 on power settings reconciles most of the popular terms.

Some ovens come equipped with a temperature probe which allows you to cook food according to its internal temperature instead of by time. It is most useful for roasting large cuts of meat. The probe needle is inserted into the thickest part of the food and the correct temperature set on the attached control. When that internal temperature is reached, the oven automatically turns off, or switches to a low setting to keep the food warm. Special microwave thermometers are also available to test internal temperature and can be used inside the oven. Conventional thermometers must never be used inside a microwave oven, but can be used outside.

A cooking guide is a feature on some ovens, either integrated into the control panel or on the top or side of the oven housing. It is really a summary of the information found in the instruction and recipe booklet that accompanies every oven. However, it does act as a quick reference and so can be a time saver.

CHART 1 Power Setting Comparison Chart

	Other Terms and Wattages	Uses
Low	ONE or TWO, KEEP WARM, 25%, SIMMER, DEFROST. 75-300 watts.	Keeping food warm. Softening butter, cream cheese and chocolate. Heating liquid to dissolve yeast. Gentle cooking.
Medium	THREE or FOUR, 50%, STEW, BRAISE, ROAST, REHEAT, MEDIUM-LOW, FIVE, 40%, MEDIUM-HIGH, SIX, 60-75%.. 400-500 watts.	Roasting meat and poultry. Stewing and braising less tender cuts of meat. Baking cakes and custards. Cooking hollandaise sauces.
High	SEVEN, FULL, ROAST, BAKE, NORMAL, 100%.	Quick cooking. Meats, fish, vegetables, biscuits/cookies, pasta, rice, breads, pastry, desserts.

Turntables eliminate the need for rotating baking dishes during cooking, although when using a square or loaf dish you may need to change its position from time to time anyway. Turntables are usually glass or ceramic and can be removed for easy cleaning. Of all the special features available, turntables are one of the most useful.

Certain ovens have one or more shelves so that several dishes can be accommodated at once. Microwave energy is higher at the top of the oven than on the floor and the more you cook at once the longer it all takes. However, these ovens accommodate larger baking dishes than those with turntables.

If you do a lot of entertaining, then an oven with a keep warm setting is a good choice. These ovens have a very low power setting that can keep food warm without further cooking for up to one hour. If you want to programme your oven like a computer, choose one with a memory control that can switch settings automatically during the cooking cycle.

Browning elements are now available built into microwave ovens. They look and operate much the same as conventional electric grills. If you already have a grill, you probably don't need a browning element. Some of the most recent ovens allow the browning element to be used at the same time as the microwave setting, which is a plus.

Combination ovens seem to be the answer to the problem of browning in a microwave oven. While the power settings go by different names in different models, generally there is a setting for microwave cooking alone, a convection setting with conventional electric heat and a setting which combines the two for almost the speed of microwave cooking with the browning ability of convection heat. However, the wattage is usually lower than in standard microwave ovens, and so cooking time will be slightly longer.

On combination settings, use recipes developed for microwave ovens, but follow the instructions with your particular oven for times and settings. Some ovens have various temperature settings to choose from. Breads, poultry, meat and pastries brown beautifully in these ovens, and conventional baking dishes, even metal, can be used with a special insulating mat. Beware of certain plastics though, as they can melt in a combination oven.

You can have your microwave oven built into the same unit as your conventional oven. Microwave ovens are best situated at eye level. In fact, there are now units available with gas or electric cooktops and a microwave oven underneath where the conventional oven used to be.

Safety and Cleaning

One of the questions most commonly asked is "Are microwave ovens safe to use?" They are safe because they have safety features built into them and they go through rigorous tests by their manufacturers and by independent agencies.

If you look at a number of microwave ovens you will see that the majority of them are lined with metal, and metal will not allow microwaves to pass through. The doors have special seals to keep the microwaves inside the oven and have cut-out devices to cut off microwave energy immediately the door is opened. There are no pans to upset, no open flames or hot elements and the interior of the oven stays cool enough to touch. Although microwave ovens don't heat baking dishes, the heat generated by the cooking food does, so it is a good idea to use oven gloves or pot holders to remove dishes from the oven. It is wise periodically to check the door of your oven to make sure it has not been bent. Check latches and hinges, too, to make sure they are in good working order. Don't use baking dishes that are too large to allow the turntable to rotate freely; this can cause the motor to over-heat or cause dents in the oven sides and door, lowering efficiency and affecting safety of operation.

Microwave ovens are cleaner and more hygienic to cook with than conventional gas and electric ovens. Foods do not spatter as much and spills do not burn, so clean-up is faster. The turntables and shelves can be removed for easier cleaning. Use non-abrasive cleansers and scrubbers, and be sure to wipe up

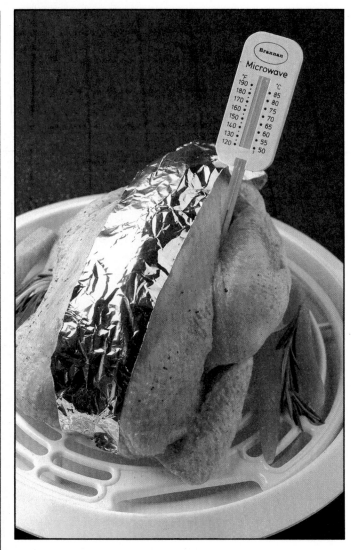

A special microwave thermometer, which is used to test the internal temperature of the food, can be used inside the oven.

Density and Shape

The denser the food, the longer the cooking time. A large piece of meat is bound to take longer to cook than something light and porous like a cake or a loaf of bread. When cooking foods of various densities or shapes at the same time, special arrangements are necessary. For instance, place the thicker part of the food to the outside of the dish, thinner part toward the middle. Arrange pieces of food in a circle whenever possible, and in a round dish. If neither of these arrangements is possible, cover the thinner or less dense part of the food with foil for part of the cooking time. Rearrange and turn over such foods as asparagus or broccoli spears several times during cooking if they will not fit into your round dishes without considerable trimming.

Size

The smaller a piece of food the quicker it will cook. Pieces of food of the same kind and size will cook at the same rate. Add smaller or faster-cooking foods further along in the cooking time, such as mushrooms to a stew. If you have a choice of cooking heights, put food that is larger and can take more heat above food that is smaller and more delicate.

Covering

Most foods will cook, reheat or defrost better when covered. Use special covers that come with your cookware or simple cover with cling film. This covering must be pierced to release steam, otherwise it can balloon and possibly burst. Tight covering can give meat and poultry a "steamed" taste. Greaseproof paper or paper towels can also be used to keep in the heat and increase cooking efficiency.

Sugar or Fat Content

High sugar or fat content in certain foods means they will absorb microwave energy faster and reach a higher temperature. It is wise to cover food that will spatter, such as bacon, and to protect cakes that have very sugary toppings.

Standing Time

Microwave recipes usually advise leaving food to stand for 5-10 minutes after removal from the oven. Slightly undercooking the food allows the residual heat to finish it off, and microwave recipes take this into consideration. Meat and baked potatoes are usually wrapped in foil to contain the heat. Standing time also makes meat easier to carve. Cakes, breads and pastries should be left on a flat surface for their standing time as this helps to cook their bases. In general, foods benefit from being covered during standing time.

any residue so that it does not build up around the door seals. Faster cooking times and lower electricity consumption combine to make microwave ovens cheaper to run, especially for cooking small amounts of food, than conventional ovens.

Once you have chosen your oven and understand what makes it work, the fun of cooking begins. There are some basic rules to remember, however, as with conventional cooking, but most of them are common sense.

Quantity

Food quantities affect cooking times. For example, one baked potato will take about 3-4 minutes, two will take about 6-7 minutes, four will take 10-11 minutes. Generally, if you double the quantity of a recipe, you need to increase the cooking time by about half as much again.

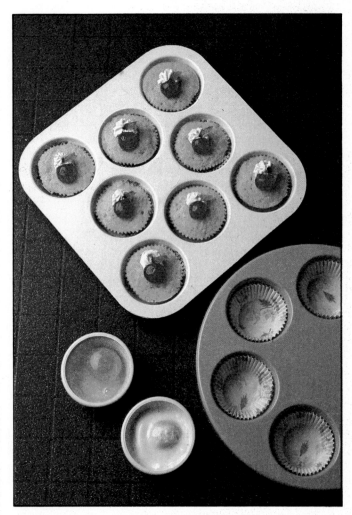

Equipment and Cookware

The number of different baking dishes and the range of equipment for microwave cooking is vast. There are so many highly specialised dishes for specific needs that to list them all would take up almost the whole of this book!

Explore cookware departments and find your own favourites. Follow your oven instruction booklet carefully since it will give you good advice on which cookware is best for your particular oven. Some dishes, lightweight plastics and even some hard plastics can't be used on combination settings. The temperature is too high and the dishes will melt or break. Most metal cookware can be used successfully in combination ovens, following the manufacturers guidelines. I have had less than satisfactory results with certain aluminium pans in my combination oven, so experimentation is essential. Paper bags can catch fire on High settings, and I have had the same experience with silicone-coated paper, although its use is often recommended. Microwave energy penetrates round shapes particularly efficiently, so round dishes and ring moulds work very well. The turntable can also be cooked on directly for such foods as scones or meringues or used for reheating foods like bread or coffee cakes.

Above and left: the number and variety of different baking dishes and the range of equipment for the microwave is vast.

For foods that are likely to boil over, like jams and soups, use the largest, deepest bowl that will fit into the oven cavity. Whole fish can be cooked in a cooking bag and curved to fit the shape of the turntable if they are too large to lie flat.

Browning dishes do work and the results are impressive. There are different designs and some have lids so that meat can be browned and finished off as a braise or stew in the same dish. Covering foods like chops or nut cutlets also speeds up the browning process. These dishes need to be preheated for between 4 to 8 minutes, depending on manufacturers instructions, and will get extremely hot. Use oven gloves or pot holders to remove browning dishes from the oven and set them on a heatproof mat to protect work surfaces. Butter will brown very fast, and steaks and chops can be seared. Stir frying is possible in a microwave oven with the use of a browning tray, and sausages brown beautifully without the shrinkage of conventional grilling or frying. These dishes can also be useful for browning a flour and fat roux for making sauces and gravies.

Cooking Poultry, Meat and Game

Moisture evaporates less readily during microwave cooking, so meat does not dry out. The fat in poultry will turn brown during cooking, but only in whole birds. Single joints of chicken or other poultry cook too quickly for the fat to brown. A thin layer of fat left on pork or beef for roasting will also brown, although it will not crisp. Fat is important to help keep the meat moist, but if you prefer to take it off, do so after cooking, or remember to baste frequently and cover the meat. There are a number of bastes, coatings and seasonings, some especially developed for microwave cooking, that can be used to give an appetizing brownness to meat and poultry.

Choose boned and rolled joints and cuts of meat that are a uniform thickness and shape. If this isn't possible, the next best thing is covering the thinner parts with foil for part of the cooking time. This trick with foil is also useful on poultry to cover the leg ends and the meat along the length of the breast bone. For poultry joints, cover the thinner ends of the breasts and the drumsticks.

Less tender cuts of meat, such as those for stewing, need to be cooked on a medium setting after initial browning. High settings can toughen these cuts of meat. Whether or not to salt

meat before cooking depends on which book you read. I think the general rules that apply to conventional meat cooking apply to microwave cooking as well. Do not salt meat to be roasted until after cooking. Sprinkle salt inside the cavity of poultry, if desired, and lightly salt stews and braises once the liquid has been added. Charts No. 2 and 3 serve as a quick reference, for meat, poultry and game.

Cooking Fish and Shellfish

The microwave oven excels at cooking fish. You can poach fish fillets in minutes. Arrange them in a dish in a circle with the thicker part of the fillet to the outside of the dish. If preparing a sauce to go with the fish, poach in a little white wine or water and lemon juice for a little more liquid to work with. A bay leaf, slice of onion and a few peppercorns are classic additions to the poaching liquid for extra flavour.

CHART 2 Meat, Poultry and Game (per 450g/1lb.)

	Mins. on High	Mins. on Medium	Internal Temperature Before Standing	After Standing
Beef: boned and rolled				
rare	6-7	11-13	57°C/130°F	62°C/140°F
medium	7-8	13-15	65°C/150°F	70°C/160°F
well-done	8-9	15-17	70°C/160°F	78°C/170°F
Beef: bone in				
rare	5	10	57°C/130°F	62°C/140°F
medium	6	11	65°C/150°F	70°C/160°F
well-done	8	15	70°C/160°F	78°C/170°F
Leg of Lamb	8-10	11-13	78°C/170°F	82°C/180°F
Veal	8-9	11-12	70°C/160°F	78°C/170°F
Pork	9-11	13-15	82°C/180°F	85°C/185°F
Ham				
Uncooked, boned	1st 5	15-18	55°C/130°F	70°C/160°F
Bone in	1st 5	15½-18½	55°C/130°F	70°C/160°F
Pre-cooked, boned	1st 5	12-15	55°C/130°F	
Bone in	1st 5	10-15		
Chicken	6-8	9-11	85°C/185°F	94°C/190°F
Duck	6-8	9-11	85°C/185°F	94°C/190°F
Turkey	9-11	12-15	85°C/185°F	94°C/190°F
Pheasant		20 total		
Poussins	15-20 total			
Wild Duck	5	10 total		
Pigeon	10 total			
Quail	5-9 total			

CHART 3 Small Cuts of Meat, Poultry and Game

Type	Mins. on High	Mins. on Medium	Special Instructions
Steaks (3.75mm/ 1½″ thick) 120g-180g/4-6oz			Use a browning dish pre-heated to manufacturer's instructions. Use timing for rare when cooking kebabs.
rare	2-3		
medium rare	3-4		
medium	5-7		
well-done	7-9		
Lamb Chops	7-9	13-15	Use a browning dish Cook in liquid
Lamb Fillet		10-12	Brown, then cook in liquid
Pork Chops	7-9	13-15	Use a browning dish Cook in liquid
Pork Fillet		15	Brown, then cook in liquid
Veal Chops	7-9	13-15	Use a browning dish Cook in liquid
Smoked Pork Chops	4-6		Pre-cooked and browned
Ham Steaks	3		Pre-cooked and browned
Minced/Ground Meat (450g/1lb)	5		Break up with a fork as it cooks
Hamburgers	2½-3		Use browning dish
Lamb Patties	2½-3		Use browning dish
Meatballs (675g/1½ lbs)	10-12		
Duck Portions 1 Breast (boned)	6		Use browning dish
2 Legs		15	Brown each side first
Chicken 1 Breast		2-3	Brown first if desired
1 Leg		3-4	
2 Pieces		3-6	
3 Pieces		4-7	
4 Pieces		7-9	
Turkey Escalopes/Cutlets		10-15	
Turkey Legs (450g/1lb)	1st 10	13-16	
Bacon		4	On rack or paper towels
		1	Per side on pre-heated browning dish
Sausages		2	Use browning dish

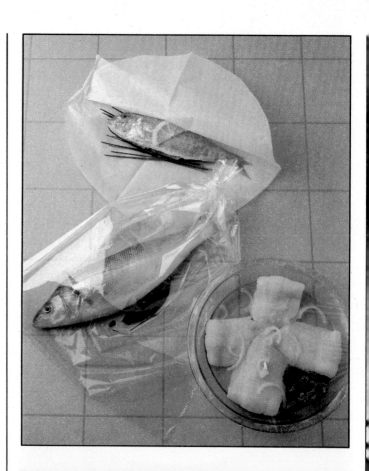

CHART 4 Fish and Shellfish (per 450g/1lb.)

Type	Mins. on high	Type	Mins. on high
Cod Steaks and Fillets	4-5	Salmon (Whole, 1kg/2.2lbs)	10-15
Halibut and Turbot Steaks and Fillets	4-5	Salmon Steaks and Tail pieces	2-7
Smoked Fish (poached)	1-2	Sea Bass (Whole, 1kg/2.2lbs)	10-15
Sole Fillets	2-3	Prawns/Shrimp Scampi/Langoustines	2-5
Mackerel	10-12	Scallops	2-5
Trout	8-10	Mussels	2-3
Herring Fillets	6-8	Oysters	1-2
Tuna Steaks	5	Squid	6
Monkfish Tail Portion	8-9		
Sliced	2-5		

Whole fish can be "fried" in a browning dish. They can also be cooked in bags, shallow covered dishes or enclosed in greaseproof paper — en papillote.

Shellfish can toughen if cooked too quickly at too high a temperature. Add them to a hot sauce and leave for 5 minutes to cook in residual heat. Alternatively, cook on their own for no more than 3 minutes.

See chart No. 4 for times and settings.

Cooking Vegetables

Microwave cooking is ideal for vegetables. Very little water is needed, so they keep their colour and nutrients. They are best cooked loosely covered, and whole vegetables like corn-on-the-cob, aubergines, artichokes and chicory can be completely wrapped in cling film and cooked without any water. Cooking bags are another alternative.

Break broccoli into even-sized pieces and, if cooking a large quantity, be sure to put the flower ends in toward the centre of the dish. Trim down the tough ends of asparagus and peel the ends of the stalks. This will help the stalks cook quickly before the tips are overcooked. Some vegetables, like cucumbers, spring onions and button onions cook very well in butter or margarine alone, if well covered. Chart No. 5 lists suggested cooking times.

Cooking Fruit

Poach, bake and preserve fruit with ease in a microwave oven. Sterilise jars for preserving by adding a little water and heating on High for about 2-3 minutes and then draining. Metal lids and rubbers seals are best sterilised outside the microwave oven.

CHART 5 Cooking Vegetables

Type	Quantity	Water	Mins. on High	Mins. Stdg. Time
Artichokes	4	430ml/¾pt/1½ cups	10-20	5
Asparagus	450g/1lb	140ml/¼pt/½ cup	9-12	5
Aubergine/ Eggplant	2 med.	30ml/2 tbsps	7-10	5
Beans Green, French	450g/1lb	140ml/¼pt/½ cup	8	3
Broad/Lima			10	3
Beetroot/Beets Whole	2	60ml/2 fl oz/¼ cup	4-5	3
Broccoli	450g/1lb	140ml/¼ pt/½ cup	4-5	3
Brussels Sprouts	450g/1lb	60ml/2 fl oz/¼ cup	8-10	3-5
Cabbage Shredded	450g/1lb	140ml/¼ pint/½ cup	7-9	3
Quartered			9-12	5
Carrots Whole	225g/8oz	140ml/¼ pint/½ cup	10	6
Sliced			7	5
Cauliflower	450g/1lb			
Whole		280ml/½ pint/1 cup	11	3
Florets		140ml/¼ pint/½ cup	7	3
Chicory	4	60ml/2 fl oz/¼ cup (water or stock)	5	3
Corn-on-the-Cob	2 ears	60ml/2 fl oz/¼ cup	6	3
Courgettes/ Zucchini	450g/1lb	60ml/2 fl oz/¼ cup	5	3
Fennel	1 bulb	280ml/½ pint/1 cup boiling water		
Sliced			2-8	3
Quartered			10-12	3
Leeks, sliced	450g/1lb	140ml/¼ pint/½ cup	7-10	3
Mushrooms	225g/8oz	30ml/2 tbsps	2	3
Okra	225g/8oz	60ml/2 fl oz/¼ cup	4	3
Onions, small	225g/8oz	30ml/1 fl oz/2 tbsps	7-8	3
Sliced	2	60ml/2 fl oz/¼ cup	10	3
Parsnips	225g/8oz	140ml/¼ pint/½ cup	8-10	3
Peas, shelled	450g/1lb	140ml/¼ pint/½ cup	10-15	5
Peapods/ Mangetout	225g/8oz	140ml/¼ pint/½ cup	3	3
Peppers	2 sliced	60ml/2 fl oz/¼ cup	3	3
Potatoes New	450g/1lb	140ml/¼ pint/½ cup	10-12	5
Baked	2		9-12	10
Boiled	450g/1lb	140ml/¼ pint/½ cup	6-7	5
Spinach	225g/8oz		4-5	3
Turnips	225g/8oz	60ml/2 fl oz/¼ cup	12	3

Paraffin wax for sealing jars cannot be melted in a microwave oven. The great advantages of microwave preserving are that jams and jellies can be made in small amounts and the job is much less messy and time-consuming. Whole preserved fruits and pickled vegetables can't be heated long enough to kill bacteria, so they must be kept refrigerated after bottling.

Cooking Rice, Pasta, Grains and Pulses

Rice and pasta need nearly as much cooking by microwave methods as by conventional ones. However, both pasta and rice cook without sticking together and without the chance of overcooking. This is because most of the actual cooking is accomplished during standing time. All kinds of rice and shapes of pasta benefit from being put into hot water with a pinch of salt and 5ml/1 tsp oil in a deep bowl. There is no need to cover the bowl during cooking, but, during standing time, a covering of some sort will help retain heat. Ease long spaghetti into the bowl gradually as it softens. Drain rice and pasta and rinse under hot water to remove starch. Both pasta and rice can be reheated in a microwave oven without loss of texture. Fresh pasta doesn't seem to take to the microwave oven successfully.

There is a great time saving with dried peas, beans and lentils — pulses. Cover them with water in a large bowl and heat on a High setting to bring to the boil, which takes about 10 minutes. Allow the pulses to boil for about 2 minutes and then leave to stand for one hour. This cuts out overnight soaking. The pulses will cook in about 45 minutes to one hour depending on what variety is used. This is about half the conventional cooking time. Make sure pulses are cooked completely; it can be dangerous to eat them undercooked. Refer to Chart No. 6 for cooking times.

Cooking Eggs and Cheese

When poaching eggs, always pierce the yolks with a skewer or fork to prevent them from bursting. Use individual ramekins or patty pans with a spoonful of water in each. Alternatively, bring water to the boil in a large dish and add a pinch of salt and 5ml/1 tsp vinegar to help set the egg whites. Slip the eggs in one at a time. Cook just until the whites are set. To stop the cooking and to keep the eggs from drying out, keep them in a bowl of cold water. For frying eggs, choose a browning dish, and for

Microwave ovens can cut the rising time for yeast doughs nearly in half, and a loaf of bread will bake in an astonishing 8-10 minutes.

Biscuits will not usually crisp in a microwave oven except in one with a combination setting. However, they bake to a moist, chewy texture which is just as pleasing. A batch of 3 dozen will cook in about 10 minutes.

Pastry is not as much of a problem as most people believe. Prick the base and sides of the pastry well, after lining a pie or flan dish. It is essential to bake the pastry shell "blind" — without filling — in order to dry the base. Pastry will not bake to an even brown. The exception is, of course, pastry baked in a combination oven. Pastry and filling can be baked at the same time in these ovens.

CHART 6 Cooking Rice, Pasta, Grains and Pulses

Type	Quantity	Water	Mins. on High	Mins. Stdg. Time
Brown Rice	120g/4oz/ 1 cup	570ml/1 pint/ 2 cups	20	5
White Rice (long grain)	120g/4oz/ 1 cup	570ml/1 pint/ 2 cups	10-12	5
Quick Cooking Rice	120g/4oz/ 1 cup	430ml/¾ pint/ 1½ cups	6	5
Macaroni	225g/8oz/ 3 cups	1 litre/1¾ pints/ 3½ cups	6	10
Quick Cooking Macaroni	225g/8oz/ 3 cups	1 litre/1¾ pints/ 3½ cups	3	10
Spaghetti	225g/8oz	1 litre/1¾ pints/ 3½ cups	6-10	10
Tagliatelle/Fettucine	225g/8oz	1 litre/1¾ pints/ 3½ cups	5-9	10
Pasta Shapes	225g/8oz/ 3 cups	1 litre/1¾ pints/ 3½ cups	6	10
Lasagne Ravioli Cannelloni	180g-225g/ 6oz-8oz	1 litre/1¾ pints/ 3½ cups	6	10
Barley	120g/4oz/ 1 cup	570ml/1 pint/ 2 cups	20	10
Bulgur (cracked wheat)	225g/8oz/ 2 cups	570ml/1 pint/ 2 cups boiling water	4	10
Dried Beans	180g/6oz/ 1 cup	1 litre/1¾ pints/ 3½ cups	55-60	10
Dried Peas	225g/8oz/ 3 cups	1 litre/1¾ pints/ 3½ cups	45-60	10
Lentils	225g/8oz/ 3 cups	1 litre/1¾ pints/ 3½ cups	20-25	15

NOTE: Add a pinch of salt and 5ml/1 tsp oil to grains and pasta

scrambling use a deep bowl or glass measuring jug. Always remove scrambled eggs from the oven while they are still very soft. Stir during standing time to finish cooking. Hollandaise sause is easy to make. Choose the same kind of container as for scrambled eggs and have a bowl of iced water ready. Use a medium setting and cook the sauce at short intervals, whisking vigorously in between times. Put the sauce bowl into the iced water at the first sign of curdling or briefly when it has thickened, to stop the cooking process.

Cheese will get very stringy if it overcooks or gets too hot. When preparing a cheese sauce, stir finely grated cheese into the hot sauce base and leave to stand. The cheese will melt without further cooking. Cheese toppings will not brown except in a combination oven. A medium setting is best for cheese.

Baking

Baking is one of the most surprising things a microwave oven does. Quick breads, those leavened with baking powder or soda and sour milk, rise higher than they do in a conventional oven and bake faster. If using a square or loaf dish, cover the corners with foil for part of the cooking time to keep that part of the bread or cake from drying out before the middle is cooked. Cakes also rise much higher and a single layer will bake in about 6 minutes on a medium setting.

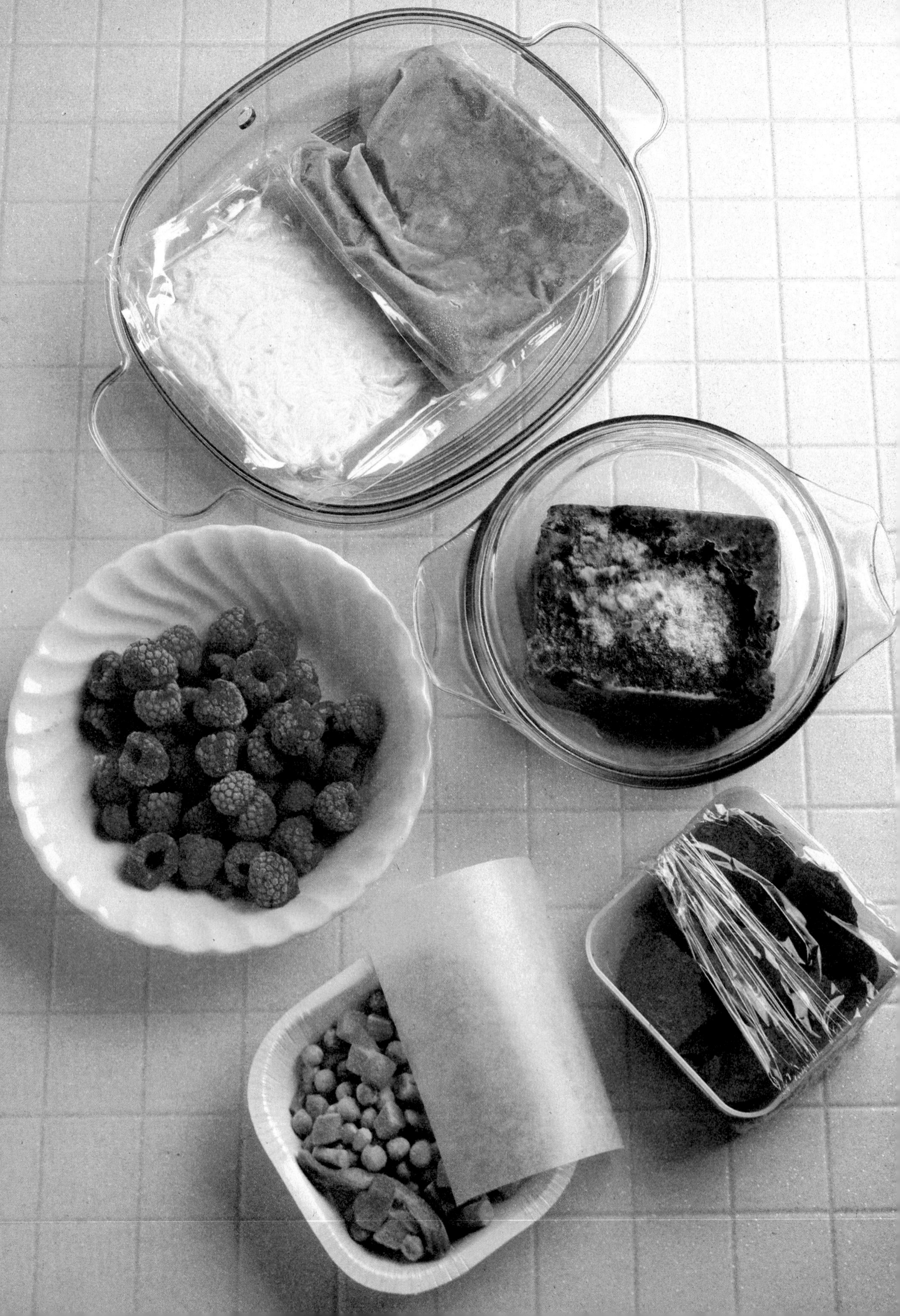

CHART 7 Reheating

	Quantity	Setting	Time from room temp. (minutes)	Special Instructions		Quantity	Setting	Time from room temp. (minutes)	Special Instructions
Spaghetti Sauce	225g/8oz 450g/1lb	Med.	5-6 7-8	Stir several times. Keep loosely covered.	Pasta	120g/4oz 225g/8oz	Med. or High	2-3 5-6	Stir once or twice. Add 5ml/ 1 tsp oil. Use shorter time for High setting.
Beef Stew	225g/8oz 450g/1lb	Med.	5-5½ 6-7	Stir occasionally. Cover loosely.	Rice	120g/4oz 225g/8oz	Med. or High	2-3 4-5	Stir once or twice. Add 5ml/ 1 tsp oil or butter. Use shorter time for High setting.
Casseroles	225g/8oz 450g/1lb	Med.	5-7 7-8	Stir occasionally. Cover loosely. Use the shorter time for chicken, fish or vegetables.	Potatoes	120g/4oz 225g/8oz 450g/1lb	High	1-2 2-3 3-4	Use the shorter time for mashed potatoes. Do not reheat fried potatoes. Cover loosely.
Chili	225g/8oz 450g/1lb	Med.	5-5½ 6-7	Stir several times. Keep loosely covered.	Corn-on-the-Cob	2 ears 4 ears	High	2-3 4-6	Wrap in plastic wrap/cling film
Pork Chops	2 4	Med.	5 7½	Turn over halfway through. Cover loosely.	Carrots	225g/8oz 450g/1lb	High	1-2 2-4	Cover loosely. Stir once.
Lamb Chops	2 4	Med.	4-5 6-10	Turn over halfway through. Cover loosely.	Turnips	225g/8oz 450g/1lb	High	1-2 2-4	Cover loosely. Stir carefully.
Sliced beef, pork, veal	120g/4oz 225g/8oz	Med.	3-5 6-7½	Add gravy or sauce if possible. Cover loosely.	Broccoli Asparagus	120g/4oz 225g/8oz	High	2 2	Cover loosely. Rearrange once.
Sliced turkey, chicken, ham	120g/4oz 225g/8oz	Med.	2½-5 4-6	Add gravy or sauce if possible. Cover loosely.	Peas Beans Courgettes/ Zucchini	120g/4oz 225g/8oz	High	1-1½ 1½-2	Cover loosely. Stir occasionally.

To let air and heat circulate underneath breads, cakes and pastry shells, place them on a rack or inverted saucer. This allows the base to cook faster and more evenly. Once baked and cool, keep microwave-baked goods well covered. They seem to dry out faster than those conventionally baked.

Defrosting and Reheating

With the defrosting and reheating abilities of a microwave oven menu planning can become crisis-free. Most ovens incorporate an automatic defrosting control into their setting programs. If your oven does not have this facility, use the lowest temperature setting and employ an on/off technique. In other words, turn the oven on at 30 second-1 minute intervals and let the food stand for a minute or two before repeating the process. This procedure allows the food to defrost evenly without starting to cook at the edges. The times given in Charts No. 7 and 8 apply to ovens of 600-700 watts.

Always cover the food when defrosting or reheating. Plastic containers, plastic bags and freezer-to-table ware can be used to freeze and defrost food in. Meals can be placed on paper or plastic trays and frozen. Cover with cling film or greaseproof paper. Usually, foods are better defrosted first and cooked or reheated second. There are exceptions to this rule, so be sure to check instructions on pre-packaged foods before proceeding. Food frozen in blocks, such as spinach or casseroles, should be broken up as they defrost.

Breads, rolls and coffee cakes can be placed on paper plates or covered in paper towels to reheat or defrost. These materials will help protect the foods and absorb moisture which will come to the surface and could make these foods soggy. If you want a crisp crust on reheated bread, slip a sheet of foil under the paper towel and don't cover completely.

When reheating foods in a sauce, stir occasionally to distribute heat evenly. Spread food out in an even layer for uniform heating. Sauces and gravies can be poured over sliced meat and poultry to keep it moist while reheating. Vegetables, except for root vegetables and starchy ones like corn, lose texture when they are reheated. It is best to add them at the last

CHART 8 Defrosting

	Mins. on Low/ Defrost Setting per 450g/1lb	Mins. Stdg. Time	Instructions		Mins. on Low/ Defrost Setting per 450g/1lb	Mins. Stdg. Time	Instructions
Pork, Veal, Lamb, Beef for Roasting	8-10	30-40	Pierce covering. Turn frequently.	Vegetables	1-8	3-5	Cover loosely. Break up or stir occasionally.
Ground/ Minced Beef or Lamb	7-8	5-6	Pierce wrapping. Break up as it defrosts.	Fish Fillets and Steaks	6-10	5-10	Pierce wrapper. Separate during defrosting. Use greater time for steaks.
Hamburgers	6-8	5	Use shorter time if individually wrapped. Pierce wrapper and separate when starting to defrost. Turn patties over once.	Whole Fish	6-8	10	Pierce wrapper. Turn over during defrosting. Cover tail with foil halfway through.
Bacon	6-8	5	Cover in paper towels. Separate as slices defrost.	Shellfish	6-8	6	Pierce wrapper. Stir or break up pieces during defrosting.
Sausages	6-8	5	Cover in paper towels. Separate as defrosting.	Bread Loaf	2-4 (per average loaf)	5-10	Cover with paper towels. Turn over once.
Whole Chickens, Duck, Game Birds	5-7	30	Pierce wrapper. Remove giblets as soon as possible. Cover leg ends, wings, breast bone with foil part of the time. Turn several times.	1 Slice Bread	20 seconds	1	Cover in paper towels.
Poultry Pieces	6-8	15-20	Pierce wrapper. Turn several times.	Rolls 6 12	1½-3 2-4	3 5	Cover in paper towels. Turn over once.
Casseroles, filled crêpes (for 4 people)	4-10	10	Defrost in dish, loosely covered. Stir casseroles if possible.	Cake	1½-2	2	Place on serving plate. Some icings not suitable.
				Fruit Pie 23cm/9″	8-10	6	Use a glass dish. Place on inverted saucer or rack.

minute to other foods. To tell if reheating is completed, touch the bottom of the plate or container. If it feels hot, then the food is ready.

Foods can be arranged on plates in advance and reheated very successfully, an advantage when entertaining. With a microwave oven, you can spend more time with your guests than by yourself in the kitchen!

Recipe Conversion

Experiment with your favourite recipes and you will probably find that many of them can be converted for microwave cooking with only a few changes. Things that don't work are recipes which call for whipped egg whites, such as angel food cake and crisp meringue shells. Soft meringues for pies will work, and one of the most amazing recipe conversions is that for crisp meringues. These meringues triple in size as they cook and are made from a fondant-like mixture.

Batters for pancakes, waffles or Yorkshire pudding are impossible to cook successfully. Deep fat frying is understandably impossible. Yeast doughs and biscuit doughs must be specially formulated for microwave cooking. To convert your own recipes, the following rules will help:

＊ Look for similar microwave recipes with the same quantities of solid ingredients, dish size, techniques and times.

＊ Reduce liquid quantities by one quarter. More can always be added later in cooking.

＊ Cut down on fat and save calories as well as cooking time. Fat will attract microwave energy and slow down the cooking of the other ingredients in the recipe.

＊ Reduce the seasoning in your recipe; microwave cooking intensifies flavours.

＊ Microwave cooking takes approximately a quarter of the time of conventional cooking. Allow at least 5 minutes standing time before checking to see if the food is cooked. You can always add more time at this point if necessary.

Microwave
THE RECIPES

Microwave
WHOLEFOOD

What are wholefoods? Simply the best ingredients with no additives, no artificial colourings, flavourings or preservatives, and with none of the essential nutrients taken away. Who eats them? Anyone who wants to combine a healthy style of eating and who enjoys eating delicious food which ranges over the cuisines of many countries.

A wholefood diet is not necessarily vegetarian, but it does make use of many interesting and perhaps slightly unusual ingredients.

The dishes tend to be high in fibre, but low in fats, salt and sugar. Wholefood meals are often lower in calories and more satisfying than their conventional counterparts. In addition, wholefoods are inexpensive to buy and, because many are dried, they are easy to store. In combination with your microwave oven, they form some of the tastiest and healthiest "convenience foods" around.

Many of the ingredients are available in your supermarket, but for more variety, browse through your local health food or wholefood shop. The variety of grains, beans, nuts, dried fruits and different flours is astonishing. One of the great pleasures of wholefood cooking and eating is discovering the enormous range of new and unusual

ingredients available. Don't be afraid to try out unfamiliar foods because you don't know how to prepare them. The basic preparation methods generally fall into only a few categories.

Most dried grains, such as rice, barley, wheatgrains and groats are first rinsed several times in cold water to remove the grain dust.

Rice and pasta need nearly as much cooking by microwave methods as by conventional ones. However, both pasta and rice cook without sticking together and without the chance of overcooking. This is because most of the actual cooking is accomplished during the standing time. All kinds of rice and all types of pasta benefit from being put into hot water with a pinch of salt and 5ml/1 tsp oil in a deep bowl. There is no need to cover the bowl during cooking but, during standing time, a covering of some sort will help retain heat. Ease long spaghetti into the bowl gradually as it softens. Drain rice and pasta and rinse under hot water to remove starch. Both pasta and rice can be reheated in a microwave oven without loss of texture.

Many of the pre-cooked grain products such as bulgur wheat and couscous, or finely ground grains such as polenta, are even quicker to prepare. These types are combined with water without rinsing, and cooked, covered in the case of bulgur wheat and couscous, or uncovered in the case of polenta, for approximately 5 minutes on HIGH. Most of the

cooking water will be absorbed. Allow them to stand for a few minutes, fluff with a fork, or give a good stir, and they are ready to form the basis of a delicious meal.

Beans require a bit more forethought, but are also easily prepared. The microwave oven offers great time savings when used to re-hydrate pulses – dried peas, beans and lentils. Cover the pulses with water in a large bowl and heat on a HIGH setting to bring to the boil, which takes about 10 minutes. Allow the pulses to boil for about 2 minutes and then leave to stand for one hour. This cuts out overnight soaking. The pulses will cook in about 45 minutes-1 hour depending on what variety is used. This is about half the conventional cooking time. Make sure pulses are cooked completely; it can be dangerous to eat them uncooked.

If you are already cooking with wholefoods, you will be pleasantly surprised to find out how the microwave can be used to speed up and improve your cooking. If you have never tried wholefoods before, you are in for a treat – delicious and healthy meals made quickly and easily, thanks to your microwave!

All the recipes in this book were prepared in an oven with a 700 watt maximum output. For 500 watt ovens add 40 seconds for each minute stated in the recipe. For 600 watt ovens add 20 seconds for each minute stated in the recipe. If using a 650 watt oven only a slight increase in overall time is necessary.

PASTA

Lasagne Rolls

PREPARATION TIME: 35 minutes

MICROWAVE COOKING TIME:
15 minutes

SERVES: 4 people

225g/8oz lasagne
5ml/1 tsp oil
340g/12oz/2½ cups cottage cheese
60g/2oz/½ cup Parmesan cheese, grated
340g/12oz/2 cups spinach, finely
   chopped
60g/2oz/¼ cup pine nuts
1 egg, beaten
2.5ml/½ tsp salt
225g/8oz/1 cup tomato purée/paste
180ml/6 fl oz/¾ cup water
10ml/2 tsps mixed herbs

Cook the lasagne, two or three sheets
at a time, in boiling water to which
you have added 5ml/1 tsp oil. Place a
few sheets in the water, microwave
for 1-2 minutes on HIGH, or until
they are just soft, but not fully
cooked. Set aside the cooked sheets
separately to prevent them from
sticking together. Cook the spinach
for 5 minutes on HIGH with no
additional water, if frozen, or 3
minutes on HIGH with a small
amount of water, if fresh. Drain and
mix into the cottage cheese. Add the
beaten egg, pine nuts, Parmesan
cheese and salt and set aside. Prepare
a sauce by combining the tomato
purée/paste with the water and
herbs. Place a large spoonful of the
cottage cheese mixture on each sheet
of lasagne and roll them up. Arrange
the rolls in a dish, and pour over the
sauce. Bake for 10 minutes on HIGH,
or until the lasagne is fully cooked
and most of the liquid is absorbed.
Check halfway through the cooking

time and add extra water if the dish
seems dry. Once you've tasted this
casserole, I'm sure you will agree that
the extra preparation time was
worthwhile.

Pasta Paprika

PREPARATION TIME: 20 minutes

MICROWAVE COOKING TIME:
13 minutes

SERVES: 4 people

340g/12oz green or wholemeal/whole-
wheat fettucini, fresh or dried

5ml/1 tsp oil
1 large onion, chopped
1 clove garlic, crushed
3 peppers, one green, one red and one
   yellow, sliced
15ml/1 tbsp olive oil
450ml/16oz can tomatoes, sieved
10ml/2 tsps paprika
60g/2oz/¼ cup Parmesan cheese, grated

**This page: Lasagne Rolls. Facing
page: Pasta Paprika (top) and
Creamy Spiced Noodles (bottom).**

Place the pasta in a large bowl, pour over boiling water to cover and add 5ml/1 tsp oil. Cook for 5 minutes on HIGH, or until the pasta is just tender. If using fresh pasta, cook for only 2 minutes on HIGH. Allow the pasta to stand in the water while you prepare the sauce. Combine the onion, garlic and sliced peppers with the olive oil and cook for 4 minutes on HIGH. Add the tomatoes and paprika. Stir this sauce into the drained pasta, sprinkle with the Parmesan cheese and cook for 4 minutes on HIGH. The red and yellow peppers add a bright note to this delicious quick supper dish, but if they are unavailable, green peppers may be substituted.

Sweet and Sour Noodles

PREPARATION TIME: 15 minutes

MICROWAVE COOKING TIME: 10-15 minutes

SERVES: 4 people

340g/12oz wholemeal/whole-wheat
  noodles
5ml/1 tsp oil
30g/1oz/2 tbsps butter or margarine
1 onion, finely chopped
1 green pepper, finely chopped
30g/1oz/2 tbsps muscovado sugar
5ml/1 tsp vinegar
5ml/1 tsp prepared mustard
2.5ml/½ tsp paprika
400g/14oz can tomatoes, chopped
4 eggs

Place the noodles in a large bowl, pour over boiling water to cover and add 5ml/1 tsp oil. Cook for 5-10 minutes on HIGH, or until the noodles are just tender. If using fresh pasta, cook for only two minutes on HIGH. Drain and set aside. Combine the onion, pepper and butter and cook for 3 minutes on HIGH to soften. Add the sugar, vinegar, spices and tomatoes and cook for a further 2 minutes on HIGH. Mix this sauce into the cooked noodles and bake for 2 minutes on HIGH. Make four indentations in the noodles with the back of a spoon and break an egg

into each. Cover the dish and microwave on MEDIUM for 1 minute, or until the eggs are set. Alternatively, prepare in individual casserole dishes.

Creamy Spiced Noodles

PREPARATION TIME: 15 minutes

MICROWAVE COOKING TIME: 11-16 minutes

SERVES: 4 people

340g/12oz wholemeal/whole-wheat
  noodles, fresh or dried
5ml/1 tsp oil
15ml/1 tbsp arrowroot
280ml/½ pint/1 cup yogurt or fromage
  frais
60g/2oz/¼ cup raisins
2.5ml/½ tsp curry powder
225g/8oz smoked fish
3 onions, finely chopped
30g/1oz/2 tbsps butter

This page: Spaghetti with Pine Nuts. Facing page: Macaroni and Blue Cheese (top) and Sweet and Sour Noodles (bottom).

Place the noodles in a large bowl, pour over boiling water to cover and add 5ml/1 tsp oil. Cook for 5-10 minutes on HIGH, or until they are just tender. If using fresh noodles, cook for only 2 minutes on HIGH. Dissolve the arrowroot in a little water and stir into the yogurt or fromage frais. Mix in the curry powder and raisins. Remove the skin and any bones from the fish and flake it. Cook the flaked fish, onions and butter for 4 minutes on HIGH. Mix in the yogurt sauce and combine with the cooked and drained noodles. Bake for 2 minutes on HIGH. Use any smoked fish you like for this quick and tasty casserole, and vary the strength of the curry powder to suit your taste!

on HIGH and stir very well. Cook for a further 2 minutes on HIGH, then stir in the blue cheese, reserving 60g/2oz/½ cup for the topping. Cook for a further 1 minute on HIGH to melt the cheese. Combine the apple, onion, garlic and oil and cook for 3 minutes on HIGH to soften. Mix into the sauce then stir in the cooked macaroni. Sprinkle the reserved cheese on top and microwave on HIGH for 4 minutes. This dish can be made with Danish Blue for more economical meals, but try using one of the luxurious Italian blue cheeses, such as Gorgonzola, for special occasions.

Spaghetti with Pine Nuts

PREPARATION TIME: 10 minutes

MICROWAVE COOKING TIME: 8-9 minutes

SERVES: 4 people

340g/12oz fresh or dried spaghetti
15ml/1 tbsp oil
1 large onion, sliced
1 clove garlic, crushed
120g/4oz/1 cup pine nuts
90ml/3 fl oz/6 tbsps olive oil
30g/1oz/¼ cup fresh parsley, chopped or 30ml/2 tbsps dried parsley
400g/14oz can artichoke hearts, drained and cut into bite-sized pieces
60g/2oz/¼ cup Parmesan cheese, grated

Place the pasta in a large bowl, pour over boiling water to cover, and add 15ml/1 tbsp oil. Cook for 5 minutes on HIGH, or until the pasta is just tender. If using fresh pasta, cook for only two minutes on HIGH. Allow to stand in the water while you prepare the sauce. Combine the onion and garlic with the olive oil and cook for 2 minutes on HIGH. Add the parsley, pine nuts and artichoke hearts and cook for a further 1 minute on HIGH. Drain the pasta, and toss in this sauce until well coated. Mix in the Parmesan cheese and serve immediately. The pine nuts and artichoke hearts make this simple pasta dish something special. Serve it with a crisp green salad for a complete meal ready in minutes.

Macaroni and Blue Cheese

PREPARATION TIME: 15 minutes

MICROWAVE COOKING TIME: 16 minutes

SERVES: 4 people

340g/12oz/wholemeal/whole-wheat macaroni
5ml/1 tsp oil
30g/1oz/2 tbsps butter or margarine
30ml/2 tbsps wholemeal/whole-wheat flour
30ml/2 tbsps arrowroot
5ml/1 tsp dried tarragon
2.5ml/½ tsp salt
570ml/1 pint/2 cups milk
225g/8oz/2 cups blue cheese, crumbled
2 apples, chopped
2 onions, sliced
1 clove garlic, crushed
15ml/1 tbsp oil

Place the pasta in a large bowl, pour over boiling water to cover and add 5ml/1 tsp oil. Cook for 5-10 minutes on HIGH, or until the pasta is just tender. If using fresh pasta, cook for only 2 minutes on HIGH. Drain the pasta to prevent it from becoming soggy. To prepare the sauce, combine the milk, butter, flour, arrowroot, tarragon and salt in a small bowl and mix well. Microwave for 2 minutes

This is a simple and quick way of preparing a baked lasagne. It produces such a light and tasty result that it is sure to become a favourite. It also makes an impressive party dish.

Spaghetti with Mussel Sauce

PREPARATION TIME: 15 minutes

MICROWAVE COOKING TIME: 7-12 minutes

SERVES: 4 people

340g/12oz wholemeal/whole-wheat spaghetti, fresh or dried
5ml/1 tsp oil

SAUCE
225g/8oz can mussels, drained
60g/2oz/4 tbsps butter
2 cloves garlic, crushed
1 onion, finely chopped
240ml/8 fl oz/1 cup white wine
30g/1oz/¼ cup fresh parsley, chopped or 30ml/2 tbsps dried parsley
4 tomatoes, peeled, seeded and cut in strips

Place the spaghetti in a large bowl, pour over boiling water to cover, and add 5ml/1 tsp oil. Cook for 5-10 minutes on HIGH, or until the pasta is just tender. If using fresh pasta, cook for only 2 minutes on HIGH. Drain and set aside. To prepare the sauce, combine the butter, garlic and onion and microwave for 2 minutes on HIGH. Add the wine, mussels and parsley and cook for a further 2 minutes on HIGH. Toss the tomatoes and cooked spaghetti in this sauce, and serve immediately. Cockles or prawns/shrimp can be substituted for the mussels, if preferred. Be sure to use only seafood which has been packed in brine, as vinegar will spoil the sauce.

This page: Spaghetti with Mussel Sauce. Facing page: Vegetable Lasagne.

Vegetable Lasagne

PREPARATION TIME: 20 minutes

MICROWAVE COOKING TIME: 15 minutes

SERVES: 4 people

225g/8oz lasagne, fresh or dried
675g/1½ lbs sliced vegetables, for example, a mixture of tomatoes, courgettes/zucchini and beans
450g/1lb/3 cups cottage cheese
120g/4oz/1 cup Parmesan cheese, grated
225g/8oz sliced mozzarella cheese
570ml/1 pint/2 cups strained fresh tomatoes
120ml/4 fl oz/½ cup water
10ml/2 tsps dried mixed herbs

Combine the strained tomatoes, water and herbs to make a sauce. Mix together the cottage cheese and Parmesan cheese, reserving 30g/1oz/¼ cup Parmesan for the topping. Pour a little of the tomato sauce into the bottom of a deep casserole dish, place 2-3 sheets of uncooked lasagne on top, followed by a thin layer of sliced vegetables, some cottage cheese and sliced mozzarella. Continue layering until the vegetables and cheese have been used up. End with a few sheets of lasagne, and pour over the remaining sauce. Sprinkle over the reserved Parmesan cheese and cook for 15 minutes on HIGH, or until the lasagne is cooked and most of the liquid has been absorbed. Check halfway through the cooking time, and add extra water if the dish seems dry. Brown under a preheated grill/broiler if desired.

Microwave
WHOLEFOOD

NUTS

Indonesian Chicken

PREPARATION TIME: 20 minutes

MICROWAVE COOKING TIME: 8-13 minutes

SERVES: 4 people

4 chicken portions, skinned or 4 boneless chicken breasts, skinned

SAUCE
2 onions, finely chopped
2 cloves garlic, crushed
30g/1oz/2 tbsps butter
225g/8oz/1 cup crunchy peanut butter
240ml/8 fl oz/1 cup water or chicken stock
15ml/1 tbsp vinegar
5-10ml/1-2 tsps chili powder, to taste
2.5ml/½ tsp salt

To make the sauce, combine the onion, garlic and butter and microwave on HIGH for 2 minutes. Mix in the remaining sauce ingredients and cook for a further 2 minutes on HIGH. Set aside while you prepare the chicken. If using chicken portions, microwave on HIGH for 8 minutes or until the chicken is fully cooked. Chicken breasts will need only 3-4 minutes on HIGH. Arrange the cooked chicken in a casserole and pour over the sauce. Microwave for 2 minutes on HIGH, or until the sauce is fully heated. This unusual sauce makes chicken into something special. Serve the chicken and sauce over rice, with green vegetables to accompany. The peanut sauce is very versatile. Serve it with other meats, or simply over a dish of mixed grains or brown rice and vegetables for a real vegetarian treat!

Sweet and Sour Peanuts

PREPARATION TIME: 15 minutes

MICROWAVE COOKING TIME: 4 minutes

SERVES: 4 people

90g/3oz/⅓ cup muscovado sugar
75ml/5 tbsps wine vinegar
45ml/3 tbsps soy sauce
15ml/1 tbsp arrowroot

This page: Indonesian Chicken. Facing page: Sweet and Sour Peanuts (top) and Curried Cashews (bottom).

1 red pepper, chopped
120g/4oz/1½ cups bean sprouts
120g/4oz/1 cup unsalted roasted peanuts
225g/8oz can bamboo shoots

Combine the sugar, vinegar, soy sauce and arrowroot and cook for one minute on HIGH. Add the remaining ingredients and microwave for 3 minutes on HIGH, or until the pepper is softened. Serve over brown rice, or Mixed Grains and Seeds for an exotic, but quickly made meal.

Stuffed Mushrooms with Sunflower Seeds

PREPARATION TIME: 10 minutes

MICROWAVE COOKING TIME: 1 minute

SERVES: 4 people

4 large flat mushrooms
125g/¼ lb smooth pâté
30g/1oz/2 tbsps sunflower seeds
Few snipped chives
30ml/2 tbsps water

Wipe the mushrooms and remove the stems. Place upside down in a dish and fill the caps with the pâté. Sprinkle the sunflower seeds and chives on top. Add the water and microwave on HIGH for 2 minutes. These stuffed mushrooms make a delightful and interesting starter to any meal. If you like, double the quantities and serve them with hot buttered wholemeal/whole-wheat toast for a meal on their own.

Curried Cashews

PREPARATION TIME: 15 minutes

MICROWAVE COOKING TIME: 9 minutes

SERVES: 4 people

1 medium onion, finely chopped
1 green pepper, chopped
15ml/1 tbsp oil
15ml/1 tbsp mustard seeds
5ml/1 tsp ground cumin
5ml/1 tsp coriander
5ml/1 tsp garam masala
225g/8oz/2 cups bean sprouts
120g/4oz/1 cup chopped or broken cashews

60g/2oz/¼ cup raisins
480ml/16 fl oz/2 cups tomato juice

GARNISH
Cucumber slices
Coriander leaves

Combine the onion, pepper and oil in a casserole for 2 minutes on HIGH. Add the spices and cook, covered, for 1 minute on HIGH. Add the nuts, raisins, bean sprouts and tomato juice and cook for a further 5 minutes on HIGH, or until the juice has thickened. Serve this nutritious and spicy dish over plain brown rice or Mixed Grains and Seeds.

Creamy Beans

PREPARATION TIME: 10 minutes

MICROWAVE COOKING TIME: 5-10 minutes

SERVES: 4 people

450g/1lb fresh or frozen green beans
2.5ml/½ tsp nutmeg
Pinch salt
30g/1oz/¼ cup slivered/shredded, toasted almonds
120ml/4oz/½ cup fromage frais or sour cream

Cook the beans in a covered casserole for 3 minutes on HIGH in 30ml/2 tbsps water if fresh, or for

570ml/1 pint/2 cups milk
120g/4oz/1 cup grated Cheddar cheese
90g/3oz/¾ cup finely chopped walnuts

Wash the cauliflower and break into flowerets. Wash and shred the cabbage. Place vegetables in a covered casserole with 6 tbsps of water and cook for 5-10 minutes on HIGH, or until the vegetables are cooked, but still slightly crunchy. Combine the butter, flour and milk in a small bowl and mix well. Cook for 4-5 minutes on HIGH, stirring well halfway through the cooking time. Add the walnuts and cheese. Combine the sauce and the vegetables and cook, uncovered for 3 minutes on HIGH. Allow to stand a few minutes before serving. This makes a delicious light lunch or supper served on its own. For a more substantial meal, try serving it on top of hot buttered wholemeal/whole-wheat toast.

Savoury Bread Pudding

PREPARATION TIME: 15 minutes

MICROWAVE COOKING TIME:
3 minutes

SERVES: 4 people

225g/8oz/2 cups wholemeal/whole-wheat or granary bread, cut into cubes
1 large onion, chopped
1 clove garlic, crushed
60g/2oz/½ cup sunflower seeds
60g/2oz/½ cup walnuts or hazelnuts, chopped
15ml/1 tbsp dried herbs
2.5ml/½ tsp salt
430ml/¾ pint/1½ cups chicken or vegetable stock

Mix together all of the dry ingredients, making sure that they are well distributed. Pour on the stock and stir to moisten. Cook, covered, for 3 minutes on HIGH. Allow to stand for a few minutes before serving. Savoury Bread Pudding is a perfect accompaniment to roast chicken. If you don't eat meat, serve it with a selection of winter vegetables such as Brussels sprouts or cabbage.

5-10 minutes on HIGH, with no additional water if frozen. Sprinkle on the nutmeg, salt, and slivered/shredded almonds, then mix in the fromage frais or sour cream. Serve immediately. This recipe makes a nice vegetable accompaniment to a grain casserole. Try it with Spinach Rice, or Lamb with Bulgur. Serve it over buttered noodles for a simple, but elegant meal.

Facing page: Creamy Beans (top) and Cauliflower and Cabbage in Walnut and Cheese Sauce (bottom). This page: Savoury Bread Pudding (top) and Stuffed Mushrooms with Sunflower Seeds (bottom).

Cauliflower and Cabbage in Walnut and Cheese Sauce

PREPARATION TIME: 15 minutes

MICROWAVE COOKING TIME:
12-18 minutes

SERVES: 4 people

1 cauliflower
1 small green cabbage

SAUCE
60g/2oz/¼ cup butter
60g/2oz/4 tbsps wholemeal/whole-wheat flour

GRAINS

Bran and Oat Meatloaf

PREPARATION TIME: 20 minutes

MICROWAVE COOKING TIME:
31-32 minutes

SERVES: 4 people

450g/1lb lean minced/ground beef
1 egg
30g/1oz/2 tbsps bran
60g/2oz/¼ cup rolled oats
1 small onion, chopped
240ml/8 fl oz/1 cup milk
5ml/1 tsp mixed dried herbs
5ml/1 tsp salt

TOMATO SAUCE
450g/1lb canned tomatoes
45ml/3 tbsps tomato purée/paste
1 clove garlic, crushed
1 onion, roughly chopped
1 green pepper, diced
15ml/1 tbsp cornflour/cornstarch
30ml/2 tbsps cold water
Salt and pepper
Sugar (optional)

Mix together all the ingredients for the meatloaf and place the mixture in a loaf-shaped dish. (Remember, if the meat is frozen you can thaw it quickly in the microwave.) Smooth the top and cook for 15 minutes on HIGH. Leave to stand for 10 minutes before turning out. To prepare the sauce, combine tomatoes and their juice, purée/paste and garlic. Cook, uncovered, on HIGH for 8 minutes or until boiling. Add the onion and green pepper and cook 5 minutes on HIGH. Combine cornflour/cornstarch with the water and stir into the sauce. Cook 3-4 minutes on HIGH, or until thickened. Season with salt and pepper and add a pinch of sugar if desired. The addition of oats and bran adds extra fibre and extra flavour to this meatloaf. You can serve it with either tomato sauce or chutney. It goes particularly well with mashed potatoes, and if there is any left over, it makes delicious sandwiches.

This page: Bran and Oat Meatloaf. Facing page: Poltenta Provençal (top) and Lamb with Bulgar (bottom).

Mixed Grains and Seeds

PREPARATION TIME: 5 minutes

MICROWAVE COOKING TIME: 20 minutes

SERVES: 4 people

120g/4oz/½ cup brown rice
60g/2oz/¼ cup wheat grains
90g/3oz/⅓ cup rye grains
90g/3oz/⅓ cup barley or oat groats
90g/3oz/⅓ cup sunflower seeds
90g/3oz/⅓ cup sesame seeds
570ml/1 pint/2 cups water
120g/4oz/1 cup grated cheese (optional)
30g/1oz/2 tbsps butter (optional)

Measure the grains and seeds into a casserole and rinse well in several changes of cold water. Cook in the water, for approximately 20 minutes, until the rice and barley are soft. Drain off any excess water and let stand, covered, for 5 minutes before serving. This dish can be easily varied by making use of other grains and seeds. It makes an excellent base on which to serve curries and tomato dishes, and makes a nice change from plain brown rice. With the addition of 120g/4oz/1 cup grated cheese and 30g/1oz/2 tbsps butter it becomes a simple supper dish on its own.

Wheat Grain Cauliflower Cheese

PREPARATION TIME: 10 minutes

MICROWAVE COOKING TIME: 10 minutes

SERVES: 4 people

1 large cauliflower
60g/2oz/¼ cup wheat grains
280ml/½ pint/1 cup water
280ml/½ pint/1 cup milk
30g/1oz/2 tbsps wholemeal/whole-wheat flour
15g/1 tbsp arrowroot
30g/1oz/2 tbsps butter
60g/2oz/½ cup grated Cheddar cheese
30g/1oz/2 tbsps grated Parmesan cheese

Wash the cauliflower, break it into

flowerets and cook it in a covered dish on HIGH for 5 minutes, using only the water that clings to the flowerets. Cook the wheatgrains in the water for 20-25 minutes on HIGH, or until they are chewy. Drain and reserve half the grains for topping. To make the sauce, combine the milk, wholemeal/whole-wheat flour, arrowroot and butter in a large bowl and stir well. Cook for 5 minutes on MEDIUM, stirring or whisking well halfway through the cooking time. Add the cheeses and the remaining wheat grains, stir well and cook for a further 2 minutes on MEDIUM, or until the cheese is melted. Pour the sauce over the cauliflower, sprinkle on reserved grains and brown under a grill/broiler if desired. For a more substantial meal, try serving this over hot buttered wholemeal/whole-wheat toast.

Polenta Provençal

PREPARATION TIME: 15 minutes

MICROWAVE COOKING TIME: 11 minutes

SERVES: 4 people

225g/8oz/1¼ cups polenta
1.1l/2 pints/4 cups water
5ml/1 tsp salt
120g/4oz/1 cup grated Cheddar cheese or 60g/2oz/3 tbsps grated Parmesan cheese
450g/1lb sliced courgettes/zucchini
450g/1lb tomatoes, roughly chopped or 400g/14oz can tomatoes
1 clove garlic, crushed or finely chopped
10ml/2 tsps dried basil
5ml/1 tsp dried oregano
2.5ml/½ tsp dried rosemary

Combine the polenta and water in a large container and cook, uncovered, on HIGH for 5 minutes. Stir very well and add the salt. Mix in the Cheddar or Parmesan cheese, and cook for a further 1 minute on HIGH. Set aside. Combine the vegetables and herbs in a separate casserole dish and cook for 5 minutes

on HIGH. Serve the vegetables on top of the polenta, with additional Parmesan cheese sprinkled on top if desired. Try substituting sliced green beans or carrots for a delicious variation when courgettes/zucchini are out of season.

Lamb with Bulgur

PREPARATION TIME: 15 minutes

MICROWAVE COOKING TIME: 16 minutes

SERVES: 4 people

450g/1lb lamb fillet, cut into chunks
1 large onion, chopped
225g/8oz/1 cup bulgur wheat
1 red pepper, seeded and cut into chunks
15ml/1 tbsp oil
430ml/12 fl oz/1½ cups chicken or lamb stock
½ tsp salt
Chopped mint
Chopped parsley

Place the onion and oil in a casserole dish and cook for 2 minutes on HIGH. Add the lamb and cook for a further 4 minutes on HIGH. Stir in the bulgur, red pepper and the stock. Cover and cook for 10 minutes on HIGH. All of the liquid should be absorbed. Let stand, covered, for 5 minutes and fluff the bulgur with a fork before serving. This is a very nice winter dish and goes well with green beans. Try it with Creamy Beans and Almonds (see recipe).

Facing page: Mixed Grains and Seeds (top) and Wheat Grain Cauliflower Cheese (bottom).

Cheese Sandwich Souffle

PREPARATION TIME: 20 minutes

MICROWAVE COOKING TIME: 21 minutes

SERVES: 4 people

8 slices wholemeal/whole-wheat or
 granary bread
15ml/1 tbsp prepared mustard
180g/6oz/1½ cups Cheddar cheese,
 grated
1 large tomato, sliced
2 large eggs, beaten
570ml/1 pint/2 cups milk
5ml/1 tsp mixed herbs
Pinch salt

Spread the mustard over 4 of the slices of bread and divide the sliced tomato and grated cheese over these slices. Use the remaining bread to cover. Place the sandwiches in a dish which they nearly fill and pour over a mixture of the beaten eggs, milk, herbs and salt. Let this mixture soak in well. Cover the dish and bake for 1 minute on HIGH, followed by 20 minutes on MEDIUM, or until the egg and milk mixture has set. Brown under the grill/broiler, if desired, before serving. Unlike a true souffle, there is no need to rush this dish to the table! It is delicious hot or cold.

Chickpeas and Bulgur Wheat

PREPARATION TIME: 10 minutes

MICROWAVE COOKING TIME: 10 minutes

SERVES: 4 people

225g/8oz/1½ cups chickpeas, cooked
15ml/1 tbsp vegetable oil
2 small onions
1 medium-sized red pepper, chopped
120g/4oz/¾ cup bulgur wheat
120ml/8 tbsps tomato purée/paste
480ml/16 fl oz/2 cups stock or water

To cook the chickpeas in the microwave, pour boiling water over them and leave to soak for at least 2 hours. Drain, then cook them in

1.1l/2 pints/4 cups of water for 25 minutes on HIGH. Cook the onion and red pepper in the oil for 2 minutes on HIGH. Add the cooked chickpeas, bulgur wheat and the tomato purée/paste dissolved in the stock. Cover and cook for 8 minutes on HIGH. Let stand, covered, for 5 minutes before serving. As an alternative you can use canned chickpeas, or chickpeas previously cooked by any other method. When pre-cooked chickpeas are used this becomes a quick and colourful main dish.

This page: Chickpeas and Bulgur Wheat. Facing page: Cheese Sandwich Souffle (top) and Mexican Rice (bottom).

Mexican Rice

PREPARATION TIME: 15 minutes

MICROWAVE COOKING TIME: 35 minutes

SERVES: 4 people

300g/10oz/1¼ cups brown rice
570ml/1 pint/2½ cups water
340g/12oz/3 cups Edam or other mild
 cheese, grated

1 120g/4oz can mild or hot chili peppers,
   to taste or 1 sweet red pepper, chopped
225g/8oz/2 cups cottage cheese
3 cloves garlic, crushed
1 large onion, chopped
2.5ml/½ tsp salt

Cook the rice in the water for 20
minutes on HIGH. Drain and mix
with the onion, chilis or red pepper,
garlic and salt. In a separate bowl mix
together the cheeses, reserving 30g/
1oz/¼ cup of the Edam for a topping.
Layer the rice and cheese mixtures in
a casserole, beginning and ending
with a rice layer. Sprinkle on the
reserved cheese and cook for 15
minutes on HIGH. Allow to stand
for 5 minutes before serving. You can
make this dish hot and spicy or mild
but tasty depending on whether you
choose to use chilis or a sweet red
pepper.

This page: Vegetable Couscous.
Facing page: Lamb Couscous.

Lamb Couscous

PREPARATION TIME: 25 minutes

MICROWAVE COOKING TIME:
30 minutes

SERVES: 6 people

450g/1lb lamb fillet, cut into chunks
2 onions, cut into chunks
1 green pepper, sliced
1 large potato, diced
4 carrots, sliced
2 small turnips, diced
225g/8oz/1 cup chickpeas, cooked (see
   below)
1 400g/14oz can tomatoes, roughly
   chopped

120g/4oz/1 cup dried apricots, chopped
5ml/1 tsp ground coriander
5ml/1 tsp ground cumin
5ml/1 tsp turmeric
5ml/1 tsp chili powder
450g/1lb couscous
850ml/1½ pints/3 cups water
5ml/1 tsp salt

Combine the lamb, onion and garlic
in a casserole and cook for 5 minutes
on HIGH. Add the rest of the
vegetables, the dried apricots, spices
and the cooked chickpeas and
microwave for a further 15 minutes
on HIGH. To cook the chickpeas in
the microwave, pour boiling water
over them and leave to soak for at
least 2 hours. Drain, then cook them
in 1.1 litres/2 pints/4 cups water for
25 minutes on HIGH. Set the stew
aside while you prepare the
couscous. Place the couscous in a
bowl with the salt and pour on the
water. Leave to stand for at least
5 minutes, until the couscous has
swollen and absorbed most of the
liquid. Cover the bowl and
microwave on HIGH for 5 minutes.
Remove the cover and fluff up the
couscous with a fork. Serve the stew
on top of the couscous. For those
who eat meat, this is a tempting
variation on the couscous theme.

Vegetable Couscous

PREPARATION TIME: 25 minutes

MICROWAVE COOKING TIME:
30 minutes

SERVES: 6 people

225g/8oz courgettes/zucchini, sliced
1 green pepper, sliced
2 onions, cut into chunks
1 large potato, diced
4 carrots, sliced
2 small turnips, diced
225g/8oz/1 cup chickpeas, cooked (see
   below)
60g/2oz/½ cup raisins or sultanas
60g/2oz/½ cup dried apricots, chopped
570ml/1 pint/2 cups water or vegetable
   stock
3 cloves garlic, finely chopped or crushed
5ml/1 tsp ground coriander

5ml/1 tsp ground cumin
5ml/1 tsp turmeric
5ml/1 tsp chili powder
450g/1lb couscous
850ml/1½ pints/3 cups water
1 tsp salt

Combine the onions, garlic, potato, carrots, turnips and green pepper in a casserole with the vegetable stock (or the water) and cook for 5 minutes on HIGH. Add the courgettes/zucchini, cooked chickpeas, raisins, apricots and spices and cook for a further 15 minutes on HIGH. To cook the chickpeas in the microwave, pour boiling water over them and leave to soak for at least 2 hours. Drain, then cook them in 1.1 litres/2 pints/4 cups water for 25 minutes on HIGH. Set the vegetable stew aside while you prepare the couscous. Place the couscous in a bowl with the salt and pour on the water. Leave to stand for at least 5 minutes, until the couscous has swollen and absorbed most of the liquid. Cover the bowl and microwave on HIGH for 5 minutes. Remove the cover and fluff up the couscous with a fork. Serve the vegetable stew on top of the couscous. Couscous is a popular dish in North Africa, where it is normally cooked by steaming over an accompanying stew. The microwave makes it quick and easy to prepare.

Herb and Cheese Cobbler

PREPARATION TIME: 20 minutes

MICROWAVE COOKING TIME: 16 minutes

SERVES: 4 people

450g/1lb/2½ cups frozen mixed
    vegetables
30g/1oz/2 tbsps butter
30g/1oz/2 tbsps wholemeal/whole-
    wheat flour
280ml/½ pint/1¼ cups milk
5ml/1 tsp arrowroot
5ml/1 tsp mixed herbs
Pinch salt

TOPPING
60g/2oz/4 tbsps butter

120g/4oz/1 cup grated Cheddar cheese
60g/2oz/1 cup bran
60g/2oz/½ cup wholemeal/whole-
    wheat flour
5ml/1 tsp baking powder
120ml/4 fl oz/½ cup milk
1.25ml/¼ tsp salt

Cook the frozen vegetables in a casserole, uncovered, for 4 minutes on HIGH. Set aside while you prepare the sauce. Place the butter, flour, mixed herbs, arrowroot, milk and a pinch of salt in a small bowl and stir well. Cook for 2 minutes on HIGH, then stir again. Cook for a further 2 minutes, then mix very well and combine with the vegetables. To prepare the topping, combine all the dry ingredients in a bowl and rub in the butter until the mixture has the texture of breadcrumbs. Stir in the milk to make a soft dough. Roll out 1cm/½ inch thick on a floured surface and cut into 8 rounds. Place the rounds on top of the filling and bake, uncovered, for 10 minutes on HIGH. Let stand for a few minutes before serving. You can also use an equivalent amount of fresh vegetables if preferred for this warming winter dish.

Vegetarian Tomale Pie

PREPARATION TIME: 30 minutes

MICROWAVE COOKING TIME: 20 minutes

SERVES: 4 people

225g/8oz/1 cup lentils, cooked or soaked
    overnight
570ml/1 pint/2 cups stock
225g/8oz/1 cup lentils, cooked
1 large onion, chopped
1 clove garlic, finely chopped or crushed
15ml/1 tbsp oil
450g/1lb fresh tomatoes, roughly
    chopped, or 400g/14oz can of tomatoes
225g/8oz/1 cup frozen sweetcorn/corn
45ml/3 tbsps tomato purée/paste
    dissolved in 280ml/½ pint/1 cup water
    or stock from the lentils
1 medium green pepper, chopped
15ml/1 tbsp chili powder
5ml/1 tsp salt

TOPPING
180g/6oz/1½ cups cornmeal
570ml/1 pint/2 cups milk
15g/½ oz/1 tbsp butter or margarine
2 eggs, beaten
5ml/1 tsp salt
225g/8oz/2 cups grated Cheddar cheese

If uncooked lentils are used, add the soaked and drained lentils to the stock and cook for 15 minutes on HIGH, until soft. Place the oil in a casserole with the onions and garlic, and cook for 2 minutes on HIGH. Add the cooked lentils, tomatoes, tomato purée/paste dissolved in the liquid, sweetcorn/corn, green pepper, chili powder, salt and water, cover and cook for 3 minutes on HIGH. Next combine the cornmeal, milk, butter and salt in a bowl and cook on MEDIUM for 5 minutes. Stir in the eggs and half of the cheese. Spread this batter over the lentil mixture, cover and bake for 10 minutes on HIGH. Sprinkle on the remaining grated cheese and cook, uncovered, for a further 2 minutes on high to melt the cheese, or brown under the grill/broiler. If you eat meat, try replacing the lentils with 450g/1lb minced/ground beef. Add the meat to the onions and garlic and cook for 5 minutes on HIGH, then proceed as normal.

Spinach Rice

PREPARATION TIME: 20 minutes

MICROWAVE COOKING TIME: 32 minutes

SERVES: 4 people

450g/1lb fresh spinach, chopped or
    450g/1lb frozen chopped spinach
1 small onion, finely chopped
340g/12oz/1½ cups brown rice
570ml/1 pint/2 cups water

Facing page: Vegetarian Tomale Pie (top) and Herb and Cheese Cobbler (bottom).

45ml/3 tbsps chopped fresh parsley, or
25ml/1½ tbsps dried parsley
2 large eggs
240ml/8 fl oz/1 cup milk
30ml/2 tbsps Worcestershire sauce
60g/2oz/4 tbsps Parmesan cheese
5ml/1 tsp salt

If using fresh spinach, wash well and chop. Cook, covered, in a large casserole for 2 minutes on HIGH, in only the water that clings to the leaves. Set aside. Frozen spinach may be placed directly in a covered casserole dish and microwaved for 5 minutes on HIGH. Wash the rice several times in cold water and cook, uncovered, in the water for approximately 20 minutes on HIGH, or until the rice is tender, but slightly chewy. Drain any excess water. Combine the eggs, milk, Worcestershire sauce, cheese and salt in a small bowl and whisk very well. Cook for 4 minutes on HIGH, stirring well after half the cooking time. Add the cooked rice and the sauce to the spinach in the large casserole dish and mix well. Cook, uncovered, for 5 minutes on HIGH. Let stand for a few minutes before serving. This dish can be served hot, but it is also delicious served cold as a colourful grain salad.

Mixed Grain Kedgeree

PREPARATION TIME: 15 minutes

MICROWAVE COOKING TIME:
24 minutes

SERVES: 4 people

90g/3oz/¼ cup brown rice
90g/3oz/¾ cup oats
90g/3oz/⅓ cup barley
90g/3oz/⅓ cup wheat grains
570ml/1 pint/2 cups water
225g/½ lb smoked fish
2 medium onions, finely chopped
60g/2oz/¼ cup raisins
30g/1oz/2 tbsps butter
Salt and pepper to taste
1 hard-boiled egg, sliced
Coriander

Remove the skin and de-bone the fish, if necessary. Flake the meat and cook with the onions, raisins and butter for 4 minutes on HIGH. Set aside. Combine the grains and cook in the water for 20 minutes, or until tender. Drain any excess liquid. Mix in the cooked fish, onions and raisins and add salt and pepper to taste. Garnish with slices of hard-boiled egg and coriander. Any combination of grains could be used as a basis for this dish. Try it using Mixed Grains and Seeds.

Spanish Barley

PREPARATION TIME: 15 minutes

MICROWAVE COOKING TIME:
26 minutes

SERVES: 4 people

340g/12oz/1½ cups barley
570ml/1 pint/2 cups water
15ml/1 tbsp oil
1 large onion, chopped

This page: **Mixed Grain Kedgeree.**
Facing page: **Spinach Rice (top)**
and Spanish Barley (bottom).

1 clove garlic, finely chopped or crushed
1 green pepper, chopped
1 400g/14oz can tomatoes, roughly
chopped
5ml/1 tsp paprika
5ml/1 tsp salt

Cook the barley in the water for 20 minutes on HIGH. Drain any excess liquid, and set the barley aside. Mix the chopped onion, garlic, and green pepper with the oil in a casserole and cook on HIGH for 2 minutes. Add the seasonings, tomatoes and the cooked barley. Cook for 4 minutes on HIGH. Let the dish stand for 5 minutes or more before serving to allow the flavour to develop. The paprika gives this dish its distinctive taste. Spanish Barley makes a colourful and tasty main dish. It can also be served cold.

PULSES

Pease Pudding

PREPARATION TIME: 1 hour

MICROWAVE COOKING TIME:
14 minutes

SERVES: 4 people

225g/½ lb/1 cup dried peas or green split
*   peas, cooked and puréed using a small*
*   amount of the cooking liquid*
1 large onion, finely chopped
1 large carrot, finely chopped
30g/1 oz/2 tbsps butter
15ml/1 tbsp arrowroot
140ml/¼ pint/½ cup milk
1 egg, beaten
2.5ml/½ tsp marjoram
2.5ml/½ tsp savory
5ml/1 tsp salt
Pepper to taste

GARNISH
Tomato slices

To cook the peas in the microwave, pour on boiling water to cover and allow to soak for at least 2 hours, or follow the instructions in the introduction for re-hydrating pulses. Microwave on HIGH for 10 minutes and 1 hour on MEDIUM or until the peas are soft. Drain, and reserve a small amount of the cooking liquid. To make the purée, either liquidize the peas in a blender or food processor, or rub them through a sieve, using the reserved cooking liquid as necessary. Mix the chopped carrot, onion, beaten egg and herbs into the purée and set aside. Combine the milk, butter and arrowroot in a bowl and mix well. Microwave on HIGH for 2 minutes and stir well. Combine with the purée and turn into a lightly-greased basin or ring mould. Cover and microwave on MEDIUM for 12 minutes. Allow to cool for a few minutes before turning out. Pease Pudding is traditionally served with bacon or ham, but if you don't eat meat, try it with a cheese omelette.

This page: Pease Pudding. Facing page: Brown Beans with Sweet Apples (top) and Succotash (bottom).

Succotash

PREPARATION TIME: 1 hour

MICROWAVE COOKING TIME:
16 minutes

SERVES: 4 people

450g/1lb/2¼ cups butter beans, cooked
450g/1lb/3 cups frozen corn
1 medium onion, chopped
1 green pepper, chopped
30g/1oz/2 tbsps butter
120ml/4 fl oz/½ cup yogurt
5ml/1 tsp arrowroot

To cook the butter beans in the microwave, pour over boiling water to cover and allow to soak for at least 2 hours, or follow the instructions in the introduction for re-hydrating pulses. Drain and cover with fresh water. Microwave on HIGH for 10 minutes and on MEDIUM for 1 hour or until soft. The butter beans may also be cooked by any other method. If canned beans are used, remember that cooked beans are approximately double the volume and weight of uncooked beans. Combine the onions and pepper with the butter, and microwave for 2 minutes on HIGH. Add the cooked beans and the frozen corn and microwave for 4 minutes on HIGH. Mix the arrowroot into 15ml/1 tbsp of the yogurt, then add the rest of the yogurt. Stir this stabilized yogurt into the beans and corn before serving. Succotash is often served with bacon, but if you don't eat meat try it with a tomato dish.

Stir-Fried Beans and Sprouts

PREPARATION TIME: 1 hour

MICROWAVE COOKING TIME:
6 minutes

SERVES: 4 people

225g/8oz/1 cup adzuki beans, cooked
225g/8oz/3 cups bean sprouts
1 onion, sliced
1 green pepper, sliced
15ml/1 tbsp oil
60ml/4 tbsps/¼ cup soy sauce

To cook the beans in the microwave, pour over boiling water and leave to soak for at least 2 hours, or follow the instructions in the introduction for re-hydrating pulses. Drain, cover with fresh water and microwave on HIGH for 10 minutes, or until the beans are soft. Alternatively, use beans cooked by any other method. Remember that cooked beans are approximately twice the weight and volume of uncooked beans. Combine the oil, sliced pepper, onion and bean sprouts and cook for 2 minutes on HIGH. Add the cooked beans and soy sauce, mix well and microwave for 4 minutes on HIGH. This is a stir-fry with a difference! Try serving it over brown rice for a complete meal.

Brown Beans with Sweet Apples

PREPARATION TIME: 1 hour

MICROWAVE COOKING TIME:
10 minutes

SERVES: 4 people

450g/1lb/2¼ cups Dutch brown beans or
   pinto beans
225g/½ lb sweet apples
225g/½ lb piece smoked bacon, cut into
   chunks
280ml/½ pint/1 cup cider or water
15ml/1 tbsp arrowroot
Salt and pepper to taste
Gravy browning

To cook the beans in the microwave, pour over boiling water to cover and allow them to soak for at least two hours, or follow the instructions in the introduction for re-hydrating pulses. Drain and cover with fresh water. Microwave for 10 minutes on HIGH and 1 hour on MEDIUM, or until the beans are soft. The beans can also be cooked by any other method. If canned beans are used, remember that cooked beans are approximately double the weight and volume of uncooked beans. Core and slice the apples, but don't peel them, and combine with the cooked beans, bacon and cider. Microwave for 10 minutes on HIGH. Make a thin paste by mixing the arrowroot with a little water and stir this into the stew. Add gravy browning for colour if desired. Cook for a further 1 minute on HIGH. Let stand for at least 10 minutes before serving to allow the flavours to develop. This stew is even tastier if made the day before and reheated for 5 minutes on HIGH. This hearty Dutch dish is traditionally served with boiled potatoes.

Garbure

PREPARATION TIME: 1 hour

MICROWAVE COOKING TIME:
23 minutes

SERVES: 4 people

450g/1lb/2¼ cups haricot beans, cooked
4 carrots, sliced
2 leeks, chopped
1 large potato, diced
850ml/1½ pints/4 cups chicken or
   vegetable stock, or water
5ml/1 tsp marjoram
5ml/1 tsp thyme
2.5ml/½ tsp paprika
Salt and pepper, to taste
1 small cabbage, shredded

To cook the haricots in the microwave, pour on boiling water and allow to soak for at least 2 hours, or follow the instructions in the introduction for re-hydrating pulses. Drain and cover with fresh water. Microwave on HIGH for 10 minutes and 1 hour on MEDIUM, or until the beans are soft. Alternatively, the beans may be cooked by any other

Facing page: Stir-Fried Beans and Sprouts.

method. Remember that cooked beans are approximately twice the volume and weight of uncooked beans. Combine the potato, carrots, leeks, haricots and stock. Cook, covered, for 20 minutes on HIGH. Spread the shredded cabbage on top, cover and cook for a further 3-4 minutes on HIGH, or until the cabbage is soft. Ladle this tasty French country stew over thick slices of wholemeal/whole-wheat bread for a hearty meal.

**This page: Bean Hotchpotch.
Facing page: Garbure (top) and
Chicken and Chickpeas (bottom).**

Chicken and Chickpeas

PREPARATION TIME: 1 hour

MICROWAVE COOKING TIME:
27 minutes

SERVES: 4 people

4 chicken portions, skins removed
225g/8oz/1½ cups chickpeas, cooked
1 large onion, finely chopped
5 cloves of garlic, finely chopped
15ml/1 tbsp oil
450g/1lb tomatoes, roughly chopped or
    400g/14oz can tomatoes, chopped
15ml/1 tbsp parsley
140ml/¼ pint/½ cup water
Salt and pepper to taste
90g/3oz okra, trimmed and sliced

To cook the chickpeas in the microwave, pour on boiling water

and allow to soak for at least 2 hours, or follow the instructions in the introduction for re-hydrating pulses. Drain and cover with fresh water. Microwave on HIGH for 10 minutes and on MEDIUM for 1 hour, or until the beans are soft. Alternatively, the beans may be cooked by any other method. Remember that cooked beans are approximately twice the volume and weight of uncooked beans. Place the onions and garlic in a casserole with the oil, and microwave on HIGH for 2 minutes. Add the remaining ingredients and cook, covered, on HIGH for 25 minutes, or until the chicken is very well cooked. Add okra during the last 2 minutes of cooking time. Serve this delicious north African stew with plenty of brown bread to mop up the juices.

Bean Hotchpotch

PREPARATION TIME: 1 hour

MICROWAVE COOKING TIME:
20 minutes

SERVES: 6 people

450g/1lb/2¼ cups haricot or other white
    beans, cooked
450g/1lb bacon, diced
450g/1lb carrots, thinly sliced
225g/½ lb parsnips, thinly sliced
225g/½ lb onions, roughly chopped
Salt and pepper to taste
10ml/2 tsps arrowroot (optional)
Parsley, chopped

To cook the beans in the microwave, pour over boiling water and leave to soak for at least 2 hours, or follow the instructions in the introduction for re-hydrating pulses. Drain and cover with fresh water. Microwave on HIGH for 10 minutes and on MEDIUM for 1 hour, or until the beans are soft. Alternatively, the beans may be cooked by any other method. Remember that cooked beans are approximately twice the weight and volume of uncooked beans. Combine all the ingredients in a large casserole and cook, covered,

for 20 minutes on HIGH, or until the vegetables are soft. If desired, the liquid can be thickened by dissolving the arrowroot in a little water. Stir this paste into the stew with the parsley and microwave, uncovered, for a further 2 minutes on HIGH. This hearty Dutch dish is really a meal in itself. Serve it with fresh wholemeal/whole-wheat rolls to soak up the juice.

Boston Baked Beans

PREPARATION TIME: 1 hour

MICROWAVE COOKING TIME: 35 minutes

SERVES: 4 people

450g/1lb/2¼ cups haricot beans, cooked
30ml/1oz/2 tbsps molasses or black
   treacle
15g/1 tbsp muscovado sugar
15ml/1 tbsp dry mustard
2 large onions, roughly chopped
225g/½ lb bacon, roughly chopped or
   1 large bacon bone
570ml/1 pint/2 cups water
2.5ml/½ tsp salt
Pepper to taste
10ml/2 tsps arrowroot (optional)

Combine the beans, bacon or bone and onions in a casserole. To cook the beans in the microwave, pour over boiling water and leave to soak for at least 2 hours, or follow the instructions for re-hydrating pulses in the introduction. Drain and cover with fresh water. Microwave on HIGH for 10 minutes and on MEDIUM for 1 hour, or until the beans are soft. Alternatively, the beans may be cooked by any other method. Remember that cooked beans are approximately twice the volume and weight of uncooked beans. Mix together the molasses, muscovado sugar, mustard powder, salt, pepper and water and pour over the beans. Add extra water if the beans are not covered. Cook, uncovered, for 35 minutes on HIGH. If desired, the sauce can be thickened by dissolving the arrowroot in a little water. Stir this paste into the beans

and microwave on HIGH for a further 2 minutes. Leave to stand for at least 10 minutes before serving, to allow the flavours to develop. This dish tastes even better when reheated. Thirty-five minutes may seem like a long time in a microwave, but it is considerably shorter than the 8-10 hours required to cook this American classic by conventional means. Try it served with Boston Brown Bread.

South American Beans and Rice

PREPARATION TIME: 1 hours

MICROWAVE COOKING TIME: 30 minutes

SERVES: 4 people

340g/12oz/1¾ cups pinto beans, cooked
340g/12oz/1½ cups brown rice
1 onion, finely chopped
1 green pepper, sliced
1 clove garlic, crushed
15ml/1 tbsp oil
850ml/1½ pints/4 cups chicken stock

To cook the beans in the microwave, pour on boiling water and allow to soak for at least 2 hours, or follow the instructions for re-hydrating pulses in the introduction. Drain and cover with fresh water. Microwave on HIGH for 10 minutes and on MEDIUM for 1 hour, or until the beans are soft. Alternatively, the beans may be cooked by any other method. Remember that cooked beans are approximately twice the volume and weight of uncooked beans. Place the onion, pepper and garlic in a casserole with the oil and cook on HIGH for 2 minutes. Add the remaining ingredients and microwave, covered, for 30 minutes on HIGH or until the rice is cooked and most of the liquid has been absorbed. For an authentic touch, serve this dish with slices of cooked banana or plantain.

Facing page: Boston Baked Beans (top) and South American Beans and Rice (bottom).

soft. Alternatively, the beans may be cooked by any other method. If canned beans are used, remember that cooked beans are approximately twice the volume and weight of uncooked beans. Mix together the cooked kidney beans, frozen sweetcorn/corn and sauce. Place this mixture in a casserole and cover with the topping. Bake, covered, for 10 minutes on HIGH. Sprinkle on the reserved cheese and cook for a further 2 minutes on HIGH. This dish may also be browned under the grill/broiler, if desired. Chili Corn Pie is a substantial meal on its own. A green salad makes a refreshing and colourful contrast.

Cassoulet

PREPARATION TIME: 1 hour

MICROWAVE COOKING TIME: 31 minutes

SERVES: 4 people

450g/1lb/2¼ cups haricot beans, cooked
450g/1lb lamb fillet, cut into pieces
2 onions, sliced
2 cloves of garlic, finely chopped
2 carrots, sliced
15ml/1 tbsp oil
450g/1lb tomatoes, roughly chopped or 400g/14oz can tomatoes, chopped
150ml/5 fl oz/½ cup red wine
1 bay leaf
5ml/1 tsp thyme
5ml/1 tsp rosemary
120g/4oz/2 cups wholemeal/whole-wheat breadcrumbs
30ml/2 tbsps bran

To cook the beans in the microwave, pour on boiling water and allow to soak for at least 2 hours, or follow the instructions in the introduction for re-hydrating pulses. Drain and cover with fresh water. Microwave on HIGH for 10 minutes and on MEDIUM for 1 hour, or until the

Chili Corn Pie

PREPARATION TIME: 2 hours

MICROWAVE COOKING TIME: 15 minutes

SERVES: 4 people

225g/8oz/1 cup red kidney beans, cooked
225g/8oz/1½ cups frozen sweetcorn/corn

CHILI SAUCE
450g/1lb tomatoes, chopped or 400g/14oz can tomatoes, chopped
1 onion, chopped
60g/2 fl oz/¼ cup wine vinegar
60g/2oz/¼ cup muscovado sugar
2.5ml/½ tsp salt
2.5ml/½ tsp cinnamon
2.5ml/½ tsp ginger
2.5ml/½ tsp mustard seeds
2.5ml/½ tsp chili powder

TOPPING
180g/6oz/1¾ cups polenta
570ml/1 pint/2 cups milk or water
15g/½ oz/1 tbsp butter or margarine
2 large eggs, beaten
225g/8oz/2 cups Cheddar cheese, grated

First prepare the topping. Combine the polenta, milk or water, butter and salt in a bowl. Add the beaten eggs and half of the grated cheese. Cook for 5 minutes on MEDIUM. Stir very well after cooking. Set aside. Next prepare the sauce by combining all the sauce ingredients. To cook the kidney beans in the microwave, cover with boiling water and soak for at least 2 hours, or follow the instructions in the introduction for re-hyrdrating pulses. Drain and cover with fresh water. Microwave on HIGH for 10 minutes and MEDIUM for 2 hours, or until the beans are

This page: Cassoulet. Facing page: Dhal (top) and Chili Corn Pie (bottom).

beans are soft. Alternatively, the beans may be cooked by any other method. Remember that cooked beans are approximately twice the volume and weight of uncooked beans. Place the oil, onions, garlic, carrots and lamb in a casserole dish and microwave on HIGH for 3 minutes. Add the beans, tomatoes, herbs and wine. Cover and cook on HIGH for 25 minutes, or until the carrots are soft. Mix together the breadcrumbs and the bran and spread over the top of the stew. Press this topping down lightly so that it absorbs some of the juice. Microwave, uncovered, for a further 3 minutes on HIGH. This is an example of wonderful French country cooking and can be made quickly and easily in the microwave.

Barbecued Beans

PREPARATION TIME: 1 hour

MICROWAVE COOKING TIME: 16 minutes

SERVES: 4 people

450g/1lb/2½ cups haricot or kidney beans, cooked
225g/½ lb Frankfurters or saveloys cut into thick slices
60g/2oz/¼ cup muscovado sugar
450g/1lb tomatoes, roughly chopped or 400g/14oz can tomatoes
30ml/2 tbsps Worcestershire sauce
2.5-5ml/½-1 tsp chili powder, to taste
5ml/1 tsp mustard powder
5ml/1 tsp salt
2.5ml/½ tsp pepper
5ml/1 tsp arrowroot

To cook the beans in the microwave, pour over boiling water and allow to soak for at least 2 hours, or follow the instructions in the introduction for re-hydrating pulses. Drain and cover with fresh water. Microwave on HIGH for 10 minutes and on MEDIUM for 1 hour, or until the beans are soft. Alternatively, use beans cooked by any other method. Remember that cooked beans are

approximately twice the volume and weight of uncooked beans. Combine all the ingredients, except for the arrowroot, in a casserole and bake for 15 minutes on HIGH. Make a paste by dissolving the arrowroot in a little water and stir this into the beans. Microwave for a further minute on HIGH. Allow to stand for at least 10 minutes before serving, to allow the flavours to develop. Barbecued Beans is a good dish to make in advance, it freezes well and the flavour is even better when defrosted and reheated in the microwave.

Tuna Butter Bean Bake

PREPARATION TIME: 1 hour

MICROWAVE COOKING TIME: 9 minutes

SERVES: 4 people

450g/1lb/2¼ cups butter beans, cooked
180g/6oz can tuna, drained
225g/8oz/1½ cups frozen peas
280ml/½ pint/1¼ cups milk
30g/1oz/2 tbsps wholemeal/whole-wheat flour
10ml/2 tsps arrowroot
30g/1oz/2 tbsps butter or margarine
120g/4oz/1 cup Cheddar cheese, grated

To cook the butter beans in the microwave, pour over boiling water to cover and leave to soak for at least 2 hours, or follow instructions in the introduction for re-hydrating pulses. Drain and cover with fresh water. Microwave on HIGH for 20 minutes and on MEDIUM for 1 hour, or until the beans are soft. Alternatively, beans cooked by any other method may be used. Remember that cooked beans are approximately twice the volume and weight of uncooked beans. Combine the cooked butter beans, drained tuna and frozen peas in a casserole. Prepare a sauce by combining the milk, arrowroot, butter and half of the grated cheese in a bowl. Microwave on HIGH for 2 minutes, stir very well and cook for a further 2 minutes on HIGH. Mix

this sauce into the beans, sprinkle the reserved cheese on top and bake for 5 minutes on HIGH. You can substitute other frozen vegetables for the peas if you wish. Try this dish with sweetcorn/corn for a tasty variation.

Dhal

PREPARATION TIME: 50 minutes

MICROWAVE COOKING TIME: 4 minutes

SERVES: 4 people

225g/8oz/1 cup red lentils, cooked
1 small onion, chopped
1 clove garlic, crushed
60ml/2 fl oz/¼ cup oil
5ml/1 tsp coriander
5ml/1 tsp turmeric
5ml/1 tsp fenugreek
2.5ml/½ tsp cumin
2.5ml/½ tsp chili powder
15ml/1 tbsp wine vinegar

To cook the lentils in the microwave, pour over boiling water to cover and soak for at least 15 minutes. Drain and cover with 700ml/1¼ pints/ 3 cups fresh water. Microwave on HIGH for 15 minutes and on MEDIUM for 50 minutes, or until the lentils are soft. Drain any excess liquid. Combine the onion, garlic and oil and cook for 2 minutes on HIGH. Mix in spices and vinegar to form a thick paste. Add the cooked lentils and stir well. Microwave for 4 minutes on HIGH. Allow to stand for 5 minutes before serving, to allow the flavours to develop. This is a delicious spicy version of an Indian classic. Serve it with warm pitta bread or, for a more substantial meal, try it over brown rice with a spoonful of natural yogurt and chopped spring/green onions on top.

Facing page: Barbecued Beans (top) and Tuna Butter Bean Bake (bottom).

Fresh and Dried Beans Provençal

PREPARATION TIME: 1 hour

MICROWAVE COOKING TIME: 7 minutes

SERVES: 4 people

225g/8oz/1 cup green flageolet beans, cooked
450g/1lb/3 cups fresh or frozen green beans
450g/1lb tomatoes, chopped or 400g/14oz can tomatoes, chopped
1 clove garlic, crushed
10ml/2 tsps dried basil
5ml/1 tsp dried oregano
2.5ml/½ tsp dried rosemary
Parmesan cheese, to taste

To cook the flageolets in the microwave, pour on boiling water to cover and soak for at least two hours, or follow the instructions in the introduction for re-hydrating pulses. Drain and cover with fresh water. Microwave on HIGH for 10 minutes and MEDIUM for 1 hour, or until the flageolet beans are soft. Alternatively, beans may be cooked by any other method. If canned beans are used, remember that cooked beans are approximately double the volume and weight of uncooked beans. Mix all the ingredients in a casserole and cook, uncovered, for 7 minutes on HIGH, stirring once halfway through cooking time. The green beans and red tomatoes make this a colourful dish. Serve it over brown rice or cooked polenta, and pass the Parmesan cheese separately.

BAKING

Ginger Nuts

PREPARATION TIME: 20 minutes

MICROWAVE COOKING TIME:
1 minute per batch

MAKES: approximately 3 dozen

120g/4oz/½ cup muscovado sugar
180g/6oz/¾ cup butter
120ml/4 fl oz/½ cup molasses/black
  treacle
3 eggs
30ml/2 tbsps milk
10ml/2 tsps vinegar
675g/1½ lbs/4½ cups wholemeal/whole-
  wheat flour
7ml/1½ tsps soda
10ml/2 tsps ginger
2.5ml/½ tsp cinnamon
Pinch ground cloves
60g/2oz/½ cup hazelnuts, chopped

Cream together the margarine, sugar, molasses, vinegar, milk and eggs. Mix in the baking soda, salt and spices, then add the flour. Finally, stir in the chopped hazelnuts. The dough should be very stiff, add extra flour if necessary. Drop by rounded teaspoonful around the edge of a plate which has been covered with wax/greaseproof paper. Microwave, 6-8 at a time, for 1 minute on HIGH. Remove to a rack to cool. If you find your molasses as "slow as molasses in January", place the jar in the oven and microwave for 30 seconds on HIGH. You will find it much easier to handle.

Facing page: Fresh and Dried Beans Provençal. This page: Peanut Butter Bran Cookies (left) and Ginger Nuts (right).

Muesli Cookies

PREPARATION TIME: 20 minutes

MICROWAVE COOKING TIME:
2 minutes per batch

MAKES: approximately 3 dozen

120g/4oz/½ cup muscovado sugar
120g/4oz/½ cup margarine
1 egg
225g/8oz/2 cups wholemeal/whole-
    wheat flour
120g/4oz/1 cup sugarless muesli
5ml/1 tsp vanilla essence/extract
2.5ml/½ tsp baking soda
2.5ml/½ tsp baking powder
Pinch salt
60g/4 tbsps dried currants

Cream together the margarine, sugar
and egg. Mix in the baking powder,
soda, salt and vanilla, then add the
muesli, currants and flour. The dough
should be very stiff; add extra flour if
necessary. Drop by rounded
teaspoonfuls around the edge of a
plate which has been covered with
wax/greaseproof paper. Microwave
for 2 minutes on HIGH. Remove to a
rack to cool. As with Sunflower
Carob Cookies, these can be baked
from frozen. Baked cookies also
freeze successfully, ready for any
unexpected guests.

Date Walnut Cake

PREPARATION TIME: 15 minutes

MICROWAVE COOKING TIME:
8 minutes

MAKES: 1 loaf

120g/4oz/1 cup sugarless dates, chopped
90g/3oz/6 tbsps margarine
140ml/¼ pint/½ cup water
120g/4oz/1 cup wholemeal/whole-
    wheat flour
10ml/2 tsps baking powder
2.5ml/½ tsp baking soda
60g/2oz/½ cup walnuts, chopped
5ml/1 tsp cinnamon
60ml/4 tbsps demerara sugar

Place the water, margarine, cut into
pieces, and the dates in a bowl and

microwave on HIGH for 3 minutes.
Mash the dates with a fork, then stir
in the remaining ingredients. Cook in
the loaf dish, which has been lined
with wax/greaseproof paper, for
5 minutes on MEDIUM. Allow to
cool for 5 minutes, then turn out
onto a rack to finish cooling. Sprinkle

with demerara sugar before leaving to
cool. Serve in slices with coffee or
tea.

**This page: Date Walnut Cake.
Facing page: Muesli Cookies (top)
and Flapjacks (bottom).**

Banana Bran Bread

PREPARATION TIME: 20 minutes

MICROWAVE COOKING TIME:
12 minutes

MAKES: 1 loaf

120g/4oz/½ cup butter or margarine
120g/4oz/½ cup muscovado sugar
2 medium eggs
2 large, very ripe bananas, mashed
60ml/2 fl oz/¼ cup plain yogurt
60g/2oz/1 cup bran
180g/6oz/1½ cups wholemeal/whole-
   wheat flour
5ml/1 tsp baking powder
2.5ml/½ tsp baking soda
2.5ml/½ tsp salt
30g/1oz/½ cup toasted bran

Cream together the butter or
margarine and sugar. Add the eggs,
mashed bananas and yogurt. Mix in
the baking powder, baking soda and
salt, and stir in the bran and flour.
Mix thoroughly. Turn the batter into
a lightly greased loaf dish. Cover the
top loosely with cling film/plastic
wrap and cover the sides of the dish
with aluminium foil, shiny side out.
Cook in the microwave for 10
minutes on HIGH. Remove the foil,
sprinkle on toasted bran, and cook
for a further 2 minutes on HIGH.
Remove the cling film/plastic wrap
and leave the loaf to cool in the dish
for 10 minutes before turning out.
This tea bread is particularly
delicious served cold, sliced and
spread with fresh butter.

Flapjacks

PREPARATION TIME: 10 minutes

MICROWAVE COOKING TIME:
4 minutes

MAKES: 16 wedges

120g/4oz/½ cup margarine
30ml/2 tbsps honey
90g/3oz/¾ cup wholemeal/whole-
   wheat flour
150g/5oz/1¾ cups rolled oats
30g/1oz/¼ cup sesame seeds

5ml/1 tsp cinnamon

Place the margarine in a mixing bowl
and cook for 2 minutes on HIGH to
melt. Mix in the honey and the dry
ingredients. Pat the mixture onto a
dinner plate which has been covered
with wax/greaseproof paper. It
should be at least 1.25cm/½ inch
thick. Bake for 2½ minutes on HIGH.
Cut into 16 wedges while still warm.
Leave the flapjacks to cool before
serving, otherwise they will crumble.
If they do, all is not lost because
flapjack crumbs make a very nice
crumble topping for fruit.

Boston Brown Bread

PREPARATION TIME: 15 minutes

MICROWAVE COOKING TIME:
8-10 minutes

MAKES: 1 large loaf

280ml/½ pint/1¼ cups plain yogurt
90ml/3oz/scant ½ cup molasses or black
   treacle
15g/½ oz/1 tbsp butter
60g/2oz/¼ cup raisins
70g/2½ oz/½ cup plus 1 tbsp plain/all-
   purpose flour
70g/2½ oz/½ cup plus 1 tbsp
   wholemeal/whole-wheat flour
90g/3oz/¾ cup polenta
5ml/1 tsp baking soda
5ml/1 tsp salt

Melt the butter for 1 minute on
HIGH. In a large bowl or food
processor, mix together the melted
butter, yogurt and molasses.
Combine the dry ingredients, add to
the mixture and stir well. Bake,
covered with cling film/plastic wrap,
in one or more well-greased loaf
containers, for 10 minutes on HIGH.
The bread rises quite a lot during
cooking, so fill the containers no
more than half full. Allow to cool
slightly before removing from the
containers. Serve warm, either plain
or with butter. This bread freezes
well, and can be easily reheated by
wrapping it in cling film/plastic wrap
and placing it in the microwave for

5 minutes on HIGH, if frozen, or
2 minutes on HIGH if at room
temperature. In Boston this bread is
the traditional accompaniment to
Boston Baked Beans, but it is also
good with cheese dishes or served
hot with butter as a tea bread.

Apple Spice Ring

PREPARATION TIME: 20 minutes

MICROWAVE COOKING TIME:
7 minutes

MAKES: 1 20cm/8 inch ring

450g/1lb eating apples, grated
90g/3oz/⅔ cup ground hazelnuts
120g/4oz/1 cup wholemeal/whole-
   wheat flour
30g/1oz/½ cup bran
60g/2oz/¼ cup muscovado sugar
   (optional)
1 egg, beaten
7ml/1½ tsps baking powder
5ml/1 tsp cinnamon
Pinch nutmeg
Pinch cardamom
60ml/2 fl oz/¼ cup milk

Combine the grated apples with the
dry ingredients, beat in the egg and
stir in the milk until well mixed. The
batter will be stiff. Turn into a 15cm/
6 inch ring mold. Smooth the top
and allow to stand for a few minutes
before baking for 3 minutes on
HIGH followed by 4 minutes on
MEDIUM, or until the cake is set,
but still moist. Allow to cool slightly
before turning out onto a rack to
finish cooling. This cake can be made
with or without sugar, and ground
almonds may be substituted for the
hazelnuts. Either way, it's simply
delicious!

**Facing page: Banana Bran Bread
(top) and Boston Brown Bread
(bottom).**

Sunflower Carob Cookies

PREPARATION TIME: 20 minutes

MICROWAVE COOKING TIME:
16 minutes

MAKES: 3-4 dozen cookies

225g/8oz/1 cup margarine or butter
225g/8oz/1 cup muscovado sugar
2 large eggs
60g/2oz/1 cup bran
180g/6oz/2 cups rolled oats
225/8oz/2 cups wholemeal/whole-
  wheat flour
120g/4oz/1 cup sunflower seeds
225g/8oz/2 cups carob drops (semi-
  sweet or dark chocolate drops may be
  substituted)
10ml/2 tsps vanilla essence/extract
5ml/1 tsp soda
5ml/1 tsp salt

Cream together the margarine, eggs, sugar, vanilla, soda and salt. Mix in the bran, oats and flour. The dough should be very stiff; if not, add more flour. Finally, stir in the sunflower seeds and carob drops, making sure they are well distributed in the dough. Drop the dough by rounded teaspoonfuls around the edge of a dinner plate which has been covered with wax/greaseproof paper or baking parchment. Most dinner plates will accommodate 6 cookies at a time. Bake on HIGH for two minutes. Allow to cool for a few minutes before removing to a rack to finish cooling. You can also form the dough into a 5cm/2 inch diameter log, cover with foil and freeze. Whenever you want a few cookies, simply cut off the desired number of 6mm/¼ inch thick slices and bake as described above for 2 minutes and 15 seconds. This is one way to make sure these popular cookies don't disappear at one sitting!

Fruit Cake

PREPARATION TIME: 20 minutes

MICROWAVE COOKING TIME:
16 minutes

MAKES: 1 large cake

225g/8oz/1½ cups dried mixed fruit
275ml/10 fl oz/1¼ cups apple juice
120g/4oz/½ cup butter or margarine
225g/8oz/2 cups wholemeal/whole-
  wheat flour
2 eggs, beaten
10ml/2 tsps baking powder
5ml/1 tsp mixed spice

TOPPING
Assorted glace/candied fruit
Apricot jam

Combine the fruit and the apple juice and allow to soak for at least 1 hour. Mix together the dry ingredients and rub in the butter or margarine until the mixture resembles fine breadcrumbs. Beat in the eggs and mix in the fruit and juice. Line the bottom of a deep 15cm/6 inch round dish with wax/greaseproof paper. Pour in the cake mixture and smooth the top. Let the mixture stand for a few minutes, then bake for 3 minutes on HIGH, followed by 13 minutes on MEDIUM, or until the centre is just dry. Allow to cool slightly, then turn out onto a rack to finish cooling. You will be amazed at the rich sweet flavour of this cake, made with no sugar at all! Serve it whenever a fruitcake is called for.

This page: Sunflower Carob Cookies. Facing page: Apple Spice Ring (top) and Fruit Cake (bottom).

Peanut Butter Bran Cookies

PREPARATION TIME: 20 minutes	
MICROWAVE COOKING TIME: 2 minutes per batch	
MAKES: approximately 5 dozen	

120g/4oz/½ cup muscovado sugar
120g/4oz/½ cup margarine
1 egg
225g/8oz/1 cup peanut butter
60g/2oz/1 cup bran
120g/4oz/1 cup wholemeal/whole-
  wheat flour
2.5ml/½ tsp salt
2.5ml/½ tsp soda
2.5ml/½ tsp vanilla essence/extract

Cream together the margarine, sugar, egg and peanut butter. Mix in the baking soda, salt and vanilla, then add the bran and flour. The dough should be very stiff; add extra flour if necessary. Drop by rounded teaspoonful around the edge of a plate which has been covered with wax/greaseproof paper. Flatten each cookie with the tines of a fork and microwave, 6-8 at a time, for 2 minutes on HIGH. Remove to a rack to cool. These rich and crumbly cookies are just the thing with a glass of milk. In the unlikely event of leftovers, they freeze well.

Carob Fruit Cake

PREPARATION TIME: 20 minutes	
MICROWAVE COOKING TIME: 16 minutes	
MAKES: 1 large cake	

225g/8oz/1½ cups raisins
280ml/½ pint/1 cups apple juice
175g/6oz/¾ cup butter or margarine
3 eggs
250g/9oz/2¼ cups wholemeal/whole-
  wheat flour
90g/3oz/¾ cup carob powder
10ml/2 tsps baking powder

Combine the raisins and the apple juice and allow to soak for at least 1 hour. Mix together the dry ingredients and rub in the butter or margarine until the mixture resembles fine breadcrumbs. Beat in the eggs and mix in the raisins and juice. Line the bottom of a 20cm/ 8 inch deep round dish with wax/greaseproof paper. Pour the mixture into the dish, smooth the top and allow to stand for a few minutes before baking for 3 minutes on HIGH, followed by 13 minutes on MEDIUM, or until the centre is just dry. Allow to cool for a few minutes in the dish before turning out onto a rack to complete cooling. This is a really rich and spicy sugarless fruit cake which you will be proud to serve to guests and family alike.

Citrus Scones

PREPARATION TIME: 20 minutes	
MICROWAVE COOKING TIME: 3 minutes per batch	
MAKES: 12 scones	

60g/2oz/¼ cup butter
30g/2 tbsps raw sugar
60g/2oz/1 cup bran
120g/4oz/1 cup wholemeal/whole-
  wheat flour
5ml/1 tsp baking powder
2.5ml/½ tsp cinnamon
Pinch salt
120ml/4 fl oz/½ cup milk
60g/2oz/¼ cup preserved mixed citrus
  peel

Combine all the dry ingredients and rub in the margarine until the mixture has the texture of breadcrumbs. Gradually add the milk to form a stiff dough, adding extra flour if necessary. Finally, mix in the peel. Roll out the dough on a floured surface to approximately 1cm/½ inch thick. Use a 5cm/2 inch round cutter to produce 12 scones. Place them around the edge of a dinner plate which has been covered with wax/greaseproof paper and microwave on HIGH for 3 minutes. Remove to a rack to cool. Served warm or cold, these scones are delicious for tea, and make a very nice breakfast bread as well.

Cornbread

PREPARATION TIME: 15 minutes	
MICROWAVE COOKING TIME: 13 minutes	
MAKES: 1 large round loaf	

180g/6oz/1 cup polenta or cornmeal
60g/2oz/½ cup wholemeal/whole-
  wheat flour
5ml/1 tsp baking soda
2.5ml/½ tsp salt
1 egg
30ml/2 tbsps honey
240ml/8 fl oz/1 cup yogurt

Combine the dry ingredients, then stir in the egg, honey, and yogurt. Spread into a loaf dish, the bottom of which has been lined with wax/greaseproof paper, and bake for 3 minutes on HIGH, followed by 10 minutes on MEDIUM. Turn out onto a rack to cool. This versatile and quickly made bread is the perfect accompaniment to a spicy dish like Barbecued Beans. It is equally delicious toasted and spread with butter and strawberry jam.

Facing page: Citrus Scones (top) and Cornbread (bottom).

minutes on HIGH, followed by 1 minute on MEDIUM. Allow to cool slightly, then cut into 16 squares. Remove from the dish when fully cool. These moist, cake-like brownies are an irresistible treat, and so easily made.

Carob Brownies

PREPARATION TIME: 15 minutes

MICROWAVE COOKING TIME: 7 minutes per batch

MAKES: 16 brownies

120g/4oz/½ cup margarine, cut into pieces
120g/4oz/1 cup unsweetened carob drops
4 eggs
250g/9oz/1¼ cups raw sugar
120g/4oz/1 cup wholemeal/whole-wheat flour
120g/4oz/1 cup walnuts, chopped
Pinch baking powder

Place the margarine and the carob drops in a bowl and melt on HIGH for 1-2 minutes. Allow to cool slightly, then beat in the eggs and salt. Stir in the baking powder, sugar and flour until they are just mixed. Bake in two 20cm/8 inch shallow round dishes, the bottoms of which have been lined with wax/greaseproof paper, for 5 minutes on HIGH, or until just set. Cut each brownie into 8 wedges while still warm. These rich and heavenly brownies are sure to become a firm favourite.

Hazelnut Brownies

PREPARATION TIME: 15 minutes

MICROWAVE COOKING TIME: 6-7 minutes

MAKES: 16 brownies

180g/6oz/¾ cup muscovado sugar
120g/4oz/½ cup butter or margarine
2 eggs
2.5ml/½ tsp vanilla essence/extract
90g/3oz/¾ cup wholemeal/whole-wheat flour
2.5ml/½ tsp baking powder
Pinch salt

60g/2oz/½ cup hazelnuts, chopped

Cut the margarine or butter into small pieces, place it in a bowl and melt it in the microwave for 1-2 minutes on HIGH. Stir in the sugar and allow to cool slightly, then beat in the eggs. Add the vanilla essence/extract and the dry ingredients, and finally mix in the hazelnuts. Line the bottom of a 20cm/8 inch square dish with wax/greaseproof paper and cover the corners with aluminium foil. Pour in the brownie mixture and smooth the top. Bake on a rack or on top of an inverted saucer for 5

This page: Carob Fruit Cake. Facing page: Hazelnut Brownies (top) and Carob Brownies (bottom).

Microwave

WHOLEFOOD

DESSERTS

Carob Blancmange

PREPARATION TIME: 5 minutes

MICROWAVE COOKING TIME:
5 minutes

SERVES: 4 people

60g/2oz/½ cup finely milled wholemeal/
   whole-wheat flour
60g/2oz/¼ cup raw sugar
280ml/½ pint/1 cup milk
30ml/2 tbsps carob powder
Slivered almonds, to garnish

Beat together all the ingredients in a
large bowl; the mixture will be lumpy.
Cook for 5 minutes on MEDIUM,
whisking very well after 2 minutes in
order to dissolve the carob powder.
Stir again at the end of the cooking
time and divide the mixture into four
small bowls. Decorate with slivered
almonds and leave to cool. Carob
gives this blancmange a rich and
spicy flavour. This dessert is nicest
when served chilled.

Maple Raisin Custard

PREPARATION TIME: 5 minutes

MICROWAVE COOKING TIME:
14 minutes

SERVES: 4 people

2 eggs

**This page: Carob Blancmange (left)
and Maple Raisin Custard (right).
Facing page: Muesli Baked Apples
(top) and Baked Carrot Custard
(bottom).**

570ml/1 pint/2 cups milk
45ml/3 tbsps maple syrup
60g/2oz/¼ cup raisins
Large pinch nutmeg

Beat the eggs well and whisk in the milk and maple syrup. Add the raisins and sprinkle on the nutmeg. Cook, uncovered, for 14 minutes on MEDIUM. Leave to stand for at least 20 minutes before serving. The custard will become firmer on cooling. The custard is very attractive when cooked in a clear glass bowl. For special occasions substitute cream for part of the milk. For a less rich custard, you can make this with skimmed milk.

Baked Carrot Custard

PREPARATION TIME: 20 minutes

MICROWAVE COOKING TIME: 22 minutes

SERVES: 4 people

450g/1lb/2 cups carrots, finely chopped
60ml/4 tbsps water
120g/4oz/½ cup unsugared dates, chopped
60ml/4 tbsps water
3 large eggs, beaten
430ml/12 fl oz/1½ cups milk
5ml/1 tsp cinnamon
2.5ml/½ tsp nutmeg
1.25ml/¼ tsp ginger
1.25ml/¼ tsp ground cloves
60g/2oz/½ cup chopped pistachios

Cook the carrots in a covered casserole with 60ml/4 tbsps water for 5 minutes on HIGH. Liquidize or rub them through a sieve without draining to make a purée. Cook the dates in 60ml/4 tbsps water for 2 minutes on HIGH and mash them without draining. Combine the puréed carrots, mashed dates, spices, beaten eggs and milk, then mix in the chopped pistachios. Cook, uncovered, in a shallow dish for 15 minutes on MEDIUM, or until the centre is just set. Let stand for at least 10 minutes before serving. The

carrots and dates provide the sweetness in this sugarless, spicy custard. It can be served warm or cold, but for the strongest flavour, serve lightly chilled.

Muesli Baked Apples

PREPARATION TIME: 10 minutes

MICROWAVE COOKING TIME: 3-4 minutes

SERVES: 4 people

4 large red apples
60ml/4 tbsps sugar-free muesli
30g/1oz/1½ tbsps muscovado sugar
30g/1oz/2 tbsps butter
120ml/4 fl oz/½ cup water

Wash and core the apples. Prick the skins in several places, but do not peel. Fill the cavities with a mixture of the muesli and the sugar. Place the apples in a casserole dish so that they are touching, dot the filling with butter and pour over the water. Bake, uncovered, for 3-4 minutes on HIGH, or until the apples are soft. Spoon over juices to serve. The microwave really excels at baked apples. These are delicious on their own or can be served with sweetened cream, yogurt or fromage frais.

Fruit and Bran Whip

PREPARATION TIME: 10 minutes

MICROWAVE COOKING TIME: 3 minutes

SERVES: 4 people

450g/1lb blackcurrants or plums
60ml/4 tbsps water
Raw sugar to taste
30g/1oz/½ cup bran
2 egg whites
Flaked almonds

Wash the fruit and, if using plums,

remove stones and roughly chop the fruit. Cook, covered, in the water for 3 minutes on HIGH. Liquidize or rub through a sieve without draining to make a purée. Add raw sugar to taste and mix in the bran. Whip the egg whites until they are stiff, but not dry. Fold them into the fruit and bran mixture. Do not overfold. Divide the whip into four dishes and chill before serving. Sprinkle with flaked almonds. For special occasions, this dessert looks very elegant when served in stemmed glasses.

Fresh and Dried Fruit Salad

PREPARATION TIME: 10 minutes

MICROWAVE COOKING TIME: 8 minutes

SERVES: 4 people

225g/8oz/1½ cups mixed dried fruit
240ml/8 fl oz/1 cup apple juice
2 dessert apples
1 orange

Combine the dried fruit and the apple juice in a bowl and microwave on MEDIUM for 8 minutes. Allow to cool. Wash the orange and cut four slices to use as a garnish, then peel and roughly chop the flesh. Wash and chop the apples, leaving the skins on. Combine the chopped apples and orange with the dried fruit and apple juice and chill. To serve, divide into 4 dishes and garnish each with an orange slice. This salad makes a refreshing end to a substantial meal. You can vary the fresh fruit as you wish.

Facing page: Fruit and Bran Whip.

Marmalade Bread Pudding

PREPARATION TIME: 10 minutes

MICROWAVE COOKING TIME: 14 minutes

SERVES: 4 people

6 slices wholemeal/whole-wheat bread
120g/4oz/½ cup marmalade

2 large eggs, beaten
570ml/1 pint/2 cups milk

Spread the bread thickly with the marmalade and cut it into 2.5cm/1 inch squares. Arrange the squares in a dish. Mix together the beaten eggs and milk and pour over the squares, making sure the bread is well soaked. Microwave for 14 minutes on MEDIUM, or until the milk and egg mixture is just set in the centre. Let stand for at least 10 minutes before serving. Marmalade adds both sweetness and flavour to this simple version of bread pudding. Serve it warm or cold.

This page: Fresh and Dried Fruit Salad. Facing page: Marmalade Bread Pudding (top) and Apple Tapioca (bottom).

Apple Tapioca

PREPARATION TIME: 5 minutes

MICROWAVE COOKING TIME:
8 minutes

SERVES: 4 people

90g/3oz/¾ cup tapioca
570ml/1 pint/2 cups apple juice
2.5ml/½ tsp cinnamon

Combine all ingredients in a bowl
and stir well. Cook for 8 minutes on
HIGH, stirring well halfway through
cooking time. Spoon into individual
dishes, if desired, and leave to stand
for at least 5 minutes before serving.
Apple Tapioca can be served warm
or chilled and is very tasty topped
with apple sauce or cream. This is a
simple way to prepare tapioca
without using any sugar.

Apple Gingerbread Pudding

PREPARATION TIME: 20 minutes

MICROWAVE COOKING TIME:
7 minutes

SERVES: 4 people

60g/2oz/¼ cup butter or margarine
1 large egg, beaten
120ml/4oz/½ cup molasses or black
*   treacle*
180g/6oz/1½ cups wholemeal/whole-
*   wheat flour*
625g/1½ lbs/1½ cups chopped apples
60g/2oz/¼ cup raisins
120ml/4oz/½ cup plain yogurt
2.5ml/½ tsp baking soda
5ml/1 tsp baking powder
5ml/1 tsp ginger
5ml/1 tsp cinnamon
5ml/1 tsp cardamom

Cream together the butter and
molasses, beat in the egg, baking
powder, baking soda and spices. Stir
in the yogurt and add the flour. Fold
in the chopped apples and raisins.
Cook, covered, in a lightly-greased

bowl, which is large enough to allow
for rising, for 7 minutes on HIGH.
Uncover and let stand for at least
10 minutes before turning out. Apple
Gingerbread Pudding is a sugarless
treat best served warm with a little
bit of milk or cream to pour over.
Should you have any left over, it is
also delicious sliced and buttered as a
moist teabread.

**This page: Apple Gingerbread
Pudding (top) and Apple Sauce
Streusel Pudding (bottom). Facing
page: Sugarless Baked Apples with
Dates.**

Apple Sauce Streusel Pudding

PREPARATION TIME: 20 minutes

MICROWAVE COOKING TIME: 6 minutes

SERVES: 4 people

450g/1lb apples, chopped or 480ml/
    16 fl oz/2 cups unsweetened apple
    sauce
180g/6oz/1½ cups brown breadcrumbs
180g/6oz/1½ cups rolled oats
120g/4oz/½ cup muscovado sugar
120g/4oz/½ cup butter or margarine
2 large eggs, beaten
5ml/1 tsp baking powder
8ml/1½ tsps cinnamon
2.5ml/½ tsp cardamom

If using fresh chopped apples, cook them in a covered dish for 4 minutes on HIGH. Liquidize or rub them through a sieve to make a purée. Allow the purée to cool, then mix in the beaten eggs, spices and baking powder. Set aside. In a separate bowl combine the breadcrumbs, rolled oats and muscovado sugar. Rub in the butter or margarine until the mixture has the texture of fine breadcrumbs. Fold in the apple purée, making sure that the batter is fully mixed. Cook, covered, in a lightly greased bowl for 6 minutes on HIGH. Uncover and allow to cool for at least 10 minutes before turning out. Apple Sauce Struesel Pudding would normally be cooked by steaming. Instead, the microwave is used to produce a perfect result in a fraction of the time.

Sugarless Baked Apples with Dates

PREPARATION TIME: 10 minutes

MICROWAVE COOKING TIME: 3-4 minutes

SERVES: 4 people

4 large green apples

60g/2oz/½ cup chopped, unsugared
    dates
60ml/4 tbsps sugar-free muesli
30g/1oz/2 tbsps butter
120ml/4 fl oz/½ cup apple juice

Core the apples. Prick the skins in several places, but do not peel. Fill the cavities with a mixture of the muesli and dates and place the apples in a casserole so that they are touching. Dot the filling with the butter and pour over the apple juice. Bake for 3-4 minutes on HIGH, or until the apples are soft. Although this recipe contains no sugar, the apples are delightfully sweet-tasting. They can be eaten on their own or served with cream.

Brown Bread Crumble

PREPARATION TIME: 15 minutes

MICROWAVE COOKING TIME: 5 minutes

SERVES: 4 people

225g/½ lb apples
225g/½ lb raspberries
Raw sugar to taste

TOPPING
90g/3oz/¾ cup wholemeal/whole-
    wheat breadcrumbs
90g/3oz/¾ cup rolled oats
60g/2oz/¼ cup muscovado sugar
60g/2oz/¼ cup butter or margarine
5ml/1 tsp cinnamon
2.5ml/½ tsp cardamom

Wash and slice the apples, but do not peel them. Place them in a small, deep dish and sprinkle on raw sugar to taste. Scatter over raspberries. To prepare the topping, combine the breadcrumbs, oats, muscovado sugar and spices. Rub in the butter or margarine until the mixture has the texture of fine breadcrumbs. Spread evenly on top of the apples and microwave for 5 minutes on HIGH, or until the apples are tender. Let stand for 5 minutes before serving.

This crumble can be served either warm or chilled, and is delicious on its own. Even so, you may prefer to serve it topped with cream or whipped cream. For a real treat, try it hot with a scoop of vanilla ice cream.

Molasses Rice Pudding

PREPARATION TIME: 10 minutes

MICROWAVE COOKING TIME: 25 minutes

SERVES: 4 people

150g/5oz/½ cup plus 2 tbsps brown rice,
    cooked
15ml/1 tbsp molasses or black treacle
280ml/½ pint/1 cup milk
2 eggs, beaten
60g/2oz/¼ cup raisins
5ml/1 tsp cinnamon

To cook rice in the microwave, place it in a bowl and rinse several times in cold water. Cook in 280ml/½ pint/ 1 cup water for 25 minutes on HIGH. Drain any excess liquid. Mix together the eggs, milk, molasses and cinnamon and add to the cooked rice. Stir in the raisins and bake, uncovered, on LOW for 25 minutes, or until the centre is just set. Leave to stand for at least 5 minutes before serving. This nutty and distinctive rice pudding is made without any sugar. It is good served either warm or cold.

Facing page: Tapioca with Sultanas/ Golden Raisins (top) and Molasses Rice Pudding (bottom).

Tapioca with Sultanas/ Golden Raisins

PREPARATION TIME: 5 minutes

MICROWAVE COOKING TIME:
8 minutes

SERVES: 4 people

90g/3oz/¾ cup tapioca
570ml/1 pint/2 cups milk
120g/4oz/½ cup sultanas/golden raisins
30g/2 tbsps muscovado sugar
Pinch cinnamon

Pistachio nuts, chopped

Combine all ingredients except the nuts in a bowl and stir well. Cook in the microwave for 8 minutes on HIGH, stirring well halfway through the cooking time. Spoon into 4 small dishes, if desired, and leave to stand at least 5 minutes before serving. Sprinkle with the nuts. The muscovado sugar gives this milk pudding a delicious distinctive taste. It can be served either warm, or chilled.

Peach Cobbler Cake

PREPARATION TIME: 15 minutes

MICROWAVE COOKING TIME:
12 minutes

SERVES: 4 people

1 400g/14oz can peaches, drained
30g/1oz/2 tbsps muscovado sugar
15g/½ oz/1 tbsp butter or margarine
Large pinch nutmeg

COBBLER
60g/2oz/¼ cup butter or margarine
30g/1oz/2 tbsps raw sugar
60g/2oz/1 cup bran
60g/2oz/½ cup wholemeal/whole-
    wheat flour
5ml/1 tsp baking powder
2.5ml/½ tsp cinnamon
Pinch salt
120ml/4oz/½ cup milk

Melt 15g/½ oz/1 tbsp butter or margarine in an 18cm/7 inch square or round dish for 1 minute on HIGH. Stir in the muscovado sugar and spread evenly over the bottom of the dish. Arrange the peaches on top. In a separate bowl mix together the dry ingredients and rub in the butter. Stir in the milk to form a soft dough. Spread the mixture on top of the peaches as evenly as possible and bake, uncovered, for 12 minutes on HIGH, or until the centre is just cooked. Allow to cool for 15 minutes, then carefully invert onto a plate. Serve with yogurt. Other canned or cooked fresh fruit can be substituted for the topping in this attractive and quickly prepared dessert. It is best when served warm.

This page: **Peach Cobbler Cake.**
Facing page: **Brown Bread Crumble.**

INDEX